THE BATTLE
OF JUTLAND

THE BATTLE
OF JUTLAND

A Bibliography

Eugene L. Rasor

Bibliographies of Battles and Leaders, Number 7
Myron J. Smith, Jr., Series Editor

(G
P)

Greenwood Press
New York • Westport, Connecticut • London

Library of Congress Cataloging-in-Publication Data

Rasor, Eugene L.
   The battle of Jutland : a bibliography / Eugene L. Rasor.
     p. cm.—(Bibliographies of battles and leaders, ISSN
  1056–7410 ; no. 7)
   Includes bibliographical references and index.
   ISBN 0–313–28124–6 (alk. paper)
   1. Jutland, Battle of, 1916—Bibliography.   I. Title.
  II. Series.
  Z6207.E8R38   1992
  [D582.J8]
  016.9404′56—dc20   91–24368

British Library Cataloguing in Publication Data is available.

Library of Congress Catalog Card Number: 91–24368
ISBN: 0–313–28124–6
ISSN: 1056–7410

First published in 1992

Greenwood Press, 88 Post Road West, Westport, CT 06881
An imprint of Greenwood Publishing Group, Inc.

Printed in the United States of America

♾™

The paper used in this book complies with the
Permanent Paper Standard issued by the National
Information Standards Organization (Z39.48-1984).

10 9 8 7 6 5 4 3 2 1

To
Cora, Jake, Hannah, Sam

CONTENTS

Contents   ix

ACKNOWLEDGMENTS

A number of persons and institutions generously have provided significant assistance in the preparation of this historiographical and bibliographical survey of the battle of Jutland.

Emory & Henry College and its Faculty Enrichment Fund and the James Still Fellowship for Advanced Study from the Kentucky Scholars Program of the University of Kentucky have provided financial assistance and opportunities for research.

Professor Jon Tetsuro Sumida of the University of Maryland has thoroughly reviewed the manuscript and recommended important changes and additions. That special effort has been particularly helpful and is much valued.

Appreciation is expressed to the following persons for support and assistance in a number of ways: Colin Baxter, Keith Bird, Alice Brown, Mickey Burris, James Casada, Barry Gough, the late Oron Hale, Robin Higham, Paul Kennedy, Roger Knight, the late Stephen Koss, the later Christopher Lloyd, Colby McLemore, Michael Moore, Wally Owen, Richard Pfau, Michael Puglisi, Bryan Ranft, Claire Rasor, Laura Rasor, John Roper, Dennis Showalter, Myron Smith, George Stevenson, Jon Sumida, Charles Sydnor, Joe Thompson, and David Woodward.

Likewise, appreciation is expressed to the following institutions for research assistance: in Great Britain, the British Library,

Public Record Office, National Maritime Museum Reading Room, Ministry of Defence Naval Library, the Institute of Historical Research at the University of London, the Portsmouth Public Library, and the university libraries of London, Cambridge, Oxford, Edinburgh, and East Anglia; in the United States, the Library of Congress and the George Marshall Library, Lexington, Virginia; in college and university libraries of Bowdoin, Chicago, Columbia, Duke, Emory, Emory & Henry, Furman, Georgetown, Harvard, Indiana, Kentucky, New York, North Carolina, Maryland, Old Dominion, Tennessee, Virginia, Virginia Tech, and Yale, and in libraries of the U.S. Naval Academy and the U.S. Naval War College at Newport, RI.

ABBREVIATIONS

BBC	British Broadcasting Corporation
BL	British Library
CID	Committee of Imperial Defence
DNB	Dictionary of National Biography
HMS	His or Her Majesty's Ship
HMSO	Her Majesty's Stationery Office
JRUSI	JOURNAL OF THE ROYAL UNITED SERVICES INSTITUTE
MM	MARINER'S MIRROR
MSS	manuscripts, personal papers
NIP	Naval Institute Press
NIProc	PROCEEDINGS OF THE NAVAL INSTITUTE
Ph.D.	Doctor of Philosophy
PRO	Public Record Office
UP	University Press
WWI	World War I
WWII	World War II

PART I

NARRATIVE AND HISTORIOGRAPHICAL SURVEY

Chapter 1

INTRODUCTION

PURPOSE AND FORMAT OF THE BOOK

This book, a volume in the Bibliographies of Battles and Leaders series, is a comprehensive bibliographical and historiographical survey of the battle of Jutland. It is prepared as a reference and research guide for the use of all levels of students and those interested in naval warfare and associated topics. The goal has been to incorporate all published books, monographs, official histories, government publications, dissertations, bibliographies, pertinent journals and periodicals and related articles in them, collections of unpublished personal papers, letters, diaries, and manuscripts, archival and research locations and germane holdings, published and broadcasted interviews, and even simulation and wargames associated with the battle of Jutland. Such materials are in English, German, and other Western languages. Sources appropriate to provide background information on the origins and consequences of World War I, related events leading up to this major naval battle of that war, and associated aspects of the battle are included.

The book is divided into two major parts for the user's convenience. There are a narrative section which is divided into logical chapters and an annotated bibliography section in which over

500 entries are numbered and listed, in most cases in alphabetical order using the last name of the author. The narrative portion describes, evaluates, assesses, qualifies, and integrates all of the entries into a whole, making the battle more understandable from a variety of perspectives and perceptions, British, German, and others. Such processes of analysis and critical evaluation are the essence of historical inquiry. That is historiography. Students of naval warfare at all levels should benefit from it as a guide and reference aid. The annotated bibliography provides more specific and individual additional information about each of the publications, documents, archival sources, and other resources available to the researcher.

For cross-referencing assistance, an item in the annotated bibliography is cited by number in brackets [—] in the narrative section every time that it is mentioned in that section. Such numbered citations in brackets are also found among the annotations themselves [—] when appropriate. There is a short glossary to identify the most important persons. To further help researchers at every level, an index is added at the end.

BACKGROUND OF THE BATTLE

The battle of Jutland or the battle off the Skagerrak, as the Germans called it, was the much trumpeted, much anticipated major confrontation of the battle fleets of Great Britain (the Grand Fleet) and Germany (the High Seas Fleet, sometimes written as High Sea Fleet) during World War I. The British expected a repetition of the battle of Trafalgar, a battle fought off the southwest coast of the Iberian peninsula on 21 October 1805 in which the British fleet of sailing ships-of-the-line under the command of Lord Horatio Nelson annihilated a combined French-Spanish fleet. Great Britain and the British fleet were not challenged again by any naval power for a hundred years. The next serious threat came from Germany beginning in the 1890s.

Likewise, the Germans excitedly anticipated "DER TAG," THE DAY. Since the 1890s Kaiser Wilhelm II aspired to naval and world power and he selected Admiral Alfred von Tirpitz to lead in the building of a battle fleet. Tirpitz formulated a naval strategy based on a concept called the "risk fleet" theory. That envisioned a situation whereby the German fleet of smaller numbers would inflict sufficient damage to the larger British fleet so that it was effectively neutralized. Tirpitz assumed the British would not risk such a confrontation. The war began in 1914 and there were several battles between sections of the battle fleets prior to mid-1916. But Jutland was the only occasion during the four years of warfare that such decisive action was possible. Full battle fleets faced each other out in "Blue Water," the open sea. In fact, neither scenario of a repeat of Trafalgar or DER TAG eventuated. The battle itself turned out to be something quite different from what anyone expected. There was bitter disappointment on both sides.

The battle took place over a two-day period, 31 May to 1 June 1916, chronologically in the middle of World War I. Both battle fleets were out in force. The actual confrontation of main forces of the opposing fleets began late on the afternoon of 31 May and the battle continued into the morning of 1 June 1916. The location was in the North Sea due west of the entrance to the Skagerrak and west of Jutland Bank off the coast of Denmark, the Jutland peninsula.

The pertinent commanders at Jutland or the Skagerrak were British admirals Sir John Jellicoe, commander-in-chief, and Sir David Beatty, commander of the Battle Cruiser Squadron, vs. German admirals Reinhard Scheer, commander-in-chief, and Franz von Hipper, commander of the Scouting Force. Scheer had taken over the High Seas Fleet earlier in the year and was determined to act more aggressively and thereby precipitate a battle. The kaiser headed the German government and prime minister H. H. Asquith led a coalition cabinet government in Great Britain.

Chapter 2

BACKGROUND

HISTORIOGRAPHICAL SURVEY OF ANGLO-GERMAN RELATIONS

World War I initially involved the Triple Entente vs. the Triple Alliance: Great Britain, France, and Russia vs. Germany and Austria-Hungary plus lesser powers, respectively. Leading antagonists were Britain and Germany. The line-up of sides involved a series of important events and diplomatic arrangements beginning about 1870.

The origins and causes of World War I have been one of the most expansive and controversial subjects debated by historians. The literature has accumulated, perhaps as much as on any other controversy. Hew Strachan [442] has produced an admirable, short survey of this subject.

Several pertinent volumes of a series, MAKING OF THE TWENTIETH CENTURY, effectively accomplished the purpose of historiographical review of the origins and causes of the war. The German and British volumes were respectively Berghahn [33] and Steiner [438]. The Eckart Kehr–Fritz Fischer revisionist school of historians, the formative group, and others have been described by James Sheehan [421], John Moses [309], and A.J.P. Taylor [457]. The key revisionists were Eckart Kehr, a precursor [246], Fischer himself [117], Berghahn [33], Kennedy [250], Lambi [260],

Herwig [192, 195], Bird [35], and Steiner [438]. Walter Hubatsch [220] and Jurgen Rohwer were examples of the more traditional view of German history. In these new interpretations, especially the German ones, there was inordinate emphasis placed on the domestic factors of Wilhelmian policy. Holger Herwig described aspects in a book and article on the "feudalization of the bourgeoisie" and the German naval officer corps [195, 196]. Lambi [260] was best on administration, including the "manipulative" Tirpitz and "irrational" kaiser, the development of operational plans formulated without coordination with the army, and materiel matters. Jurgen Kocka [256] has described German society as it coped with the prospect of total war.

Many writers of all persuasions have agreed that one of the primary factors contributing to the antagonism which eventually led to war was the Anglo-German naval arms race, especially from the time Germany began constructing a battle fleet in the mid-1890s until the outbreak of the war in August 1914. The personalities associated with battle fleet developments were Admiral Tirpitz for Germany and Admiral Sir John "Jacky" Fisher, first sea lord of the Admiralty for Great Britain. Among the historians who stressed the significance of the naval arms race as a contributory factor to the outbreak of the war were Oron Hale [168, 169, 170], Keith Bird [35], Paul Kennedy [250], Peter Padfield [336], and Richard Langhorne [262]. Questions about the centrality of the issue of the Anglo-German naval arms race have been raised by Charles Fairbanks [514] and Jon Sumida [449].

The individual navies have been the focus of some outstanding scholars. For the British, there were Arthur Marder [294,297], who has been the most widely acclaimed British naval historian, Stephen Roskill [390], Paul Kennedy [251], and Jon Sumida [449], all significant contributors on the naval aspects of the period before and during World War I. For the Germans, there has been no equivalent to Marder, but important monographs have been produced by Jonathan Steinberg [437], Holger Herwig [193, 196, 197], Volcker Berghahn [32, 33], Paul Kennedy [249, 250, 252], and Walter Hubatsch [219]. Eugene Rasor has reviewed the background of Anglo-German relations and assessed the contributions of the three great British historians in historiographical surveys, a book [376, pp. 33–53], and an article in the

Frank Homer anthology [207, pp. 27–60].

The best and most comprehensive study on the subject of Anglo-German relations during the decades before World War I was by Kennedy [250] in a structuralist approach, as he described it, incorporating social, economic, ideological, cultural, and domestic-political factors which influenced and in some cases dictated the courses of the foreign policies of Great Britain and Germany. Kennedy studied "the Official Mind," i.e., how and what was influencing the authorities who made ultimate decisions of peace and war. He considered comparative connections between dynasties, religion, pressure groups, and ideological trends, e.g., the kaiser's love-hate relationship toward his uncle King Edward VII, the rise of naval leagues, and the decline of liberalism in both countries. He has directly compared Fisher and Tirpitz in an article in the Jordan anthology [240, pp. 45–59].

Kennedy has also edited an anthology on pre–World War I war plans [253]. Paul Haggie did the article on war planning and the Royal Navy (pp. 118–32). Some traditional, older approaches to Anglo-German relations in the late nineteenth and early twentieth centuries were by Raymond Sontag [431] and Bernadotte Schmitt [412].

More recently, Volcker Berghahn, GERMANY AND THE APPROACH OF WAR IN 1914 [33], THE MAKING OF THE TWENTIETH CENTURY series volume, brilliantly reflected and summarized the revisionist interpretations of the most recent German scholarship on Tirpitz, the kaiser, and the development of the German battle fleet and its strategic policies. THE MAKING OF THE TWENTIETH CENTURY series volume on Great Britain was by Zara Steiner [438]. Like the Berghahn piece, it reviewed in detail the domestic, diplomatic, military-naval, and strategic factors which led to the decision of the British cabinet for war in early August 1914.

STRATEGIC DEVELOPMENTS IN
GREAT BRITAIN

The definitive history of the pre–World War I Royal Navy in all of its facets was Arthur Marder's earlier ANATOMY [294] followed by his five–volume FROM DREADNOUGHT . . .

FISHER ERA [297]. Volume III, originally published in 1966, and the only one revised, in 1978, was on Jutland. This has remained the most thorough and the most complete account of the battle. ANATOMY and the first two volumes of FROM DREADNOUGHT covered the formative years of Fisher's early career, his rise to leadership, and implementation of an extensive series of reforms. In many ways, Marder's account of Fisher and the "Fisher Era," a phrase Marder coined to describe the period from about 1890 to 1919, was a panegyric. For Jutland, Marder was partial to Jellicoe, Fisher's choice as commander-in-chief of the Grand Fleet. Marder's research and analyses were unsurpassed but not unchallenged.

Between 1902 and the outbreak of the war, British strategic policies and war planning were coordinated in theory under the oversight of a new organization, the Committee of Imperial Defence (CID), created by Prime Minister A. J. Balfour with Lord Esher and Maurice Hankey as key figures in its development. Even Fisher initially endorsed the effort, but he was quickly disenchanted. It never functioned as the much-copied Prussian General Staff of the late nineteenth century, but it was a significant institution and, on occasion, became the center of some aspects of war planning. Among the surveys of CID and pre-war strategic planning were the following: Johnson [235], D'Ombrain [96, 97], David French [121, 123], and a London dissertation by N. W. Summerton [452]. Hankey [179] has published his memoirs of World War I. Roskill's three volumes on this "man of secrets" was the definitive biography [395].

Haggie [166] has recounted a serious, if not fatal, flaw in the Fisher reform efforts, the lack of a naval or war planning staff. Sir Julian Corbett, Esher, and Sir Herbert Richmond all urged Fisher to do something about this deficiency, but to no avail. Winston Churchill was brought in as first lord of the Admiralty in 1911 also with the same mandate. A staff of sorts was created. See the article by D'Ombrain [96].

The development of naval strategic thought in Great Britain, and the most distinguished strategist, have both been comprehensively reviewed by Donald Schurman: THE EDUCATION OF A NAVY [414] and JULIAN S. CORBETT [415]. In the former, the achievements of six bold and original "historians," including

Richmond and Corbett, were analyzed; this book was followed by the biography of the man who, many declare, was the most brilliant naval strategist of all time. For some time Corbett was "in the Fishpond," but as Fisher degenerated into megalomania, Corbett increasingly became a critic. He repeatedly called for a naval staff and strategic preparation and education of naval leaders. The Corbett strategy always emphasized maintenance of lines of communications, not necessarily the constant seeking of decisive battles. Tunstall [471] has catalogued the Corbett papers.

In the Jordan anthology [240, pp. 118–27], John Slessor contributed an analysis of Admiralty command policy during World War I and World War II using Jutland as a case study. The primary problem at Jutland was the absence of higher strategic direction and leadership, and it persisted in World War II, Slessor concluded. There was "criminal neglect" on the part of the Admiralty in failure to inform Jellicoe of pertinent intelligence and other information.

An impressionistic and superficial survey of the Royal Navy from the 1830s to the 1910s, concentrating on strategic dominance—the Royal Navy "was a legendary force . . . unchallengeable . . . sea-rulers by birthright" (pp. 2–4)—and naval life, was published by Peter Padfield [338]. Padfield also wrote a novel [339] with similar descriptions and characterizations.

Three related topics have received notable attention. Marion Siney [424] presented a critical history of the Allied blockade of Germany during the first two years of World War I. She described it as economic warfare initiated by the British. Second, naval tactical doctrine, the engagement of forces in proximity, has been surveyed by Fioravanzo [516], Hughes [520], and Robison [528]. Third, British naval and strategic obligations and German and other nations' dispositions of naval forces in the Mediterranean Sea, a vital area for naval power, were brilliantly described in a series of intensively researched volumes by Paul Halpern [173, 174, 175].

STRATEGIC DEVELOPMENTS IN GERMANY

There has not been anything equivalent to Marder's "magnum

opus" [294, 297] for Germany or the German navy. One of the best analysts on this issue has been Paul Kennedy. His comprehensive study of Anglo-German relations in all aspects has been reviewed above [250]. There was also an article [252], an early one by Kennedy which won him the prestigious Julian Corbett Essay prize, on a step in Tirpitz's battle fleet development, a step Kennedy concluded was a serious error for Germany.

The chief contemporary German critic of Tirpitz's naval strategy was Wolfgang Wegener [485]. Like Corbett, he de-emphasized the significance of the decisive battle. "We never really understood the sea. Not one of us," Wegener concluded (pp. vii). Carl-Axel Gemzell [134] presented a comprehensive review of German naval strategic planning from 1888 to 1940, insisting that the issues were more complex than analysts such as Walter Hubatsch [219], Jonathan Steinberg [437], and Volker Berghahn [32] have presented them.

Holger Herwig [192, 193, 195, 196, 197] has written several analyses of German naval officers, the competition between army and navy strategists, and the development of the German navy. Herwig also wrote the assessment of German naval strategy in the Allan Millett anthology, MILITARY EFFECTIVENESS [303, vol. I, pp. 80–115]. Tirpitz formulated the strategy in 1894 and, although conditions changed drastically in Germany, the strategy remained unchanged: to annihilate the British fleet in the North Sea within 100 miles of Heligoland. At no time was there an effort to coordinate military and naval strategies. Herwig concluded: "In fact, the Royal Navy's refusal in 1914 to play the role accorded it by Tirpitz effectively ended naval strategy for Germany during the first World War." All later actions were "ad hoc tactical maneuvers." The chance meeting at Jutland failed to alter the strategic balance.

Steinberg has penned a book, YESTERDAY'S DETERRENT [437], and four articles [433, 434, 435, 436] on the development of the German battle fleet and its consequences in Germany. There was an Indiana dissertation by James Sutton [453]. The failure of German policy makers to appreciate and exploit the strategic concerns of Great Britain which related to perceived threats from Russia and Germany was the focus of Oswald Hauser [188].

THE ANGLO-GERMAN NAVAL ARMS RACE

As noted above, this competition was deemed highly significant among the origins and causes of World War I. Two early dissertations on this topic were by Samuel Halpern [171] and by Waldo Chamberlain [508]. Marder [297] has much on this subject.

An entire book was devoted to this arms race: Peter Padfield [336], who used extensive British and German sources, focused on the years 1900–1914 with lengthy sections on Tirpitz and the development of the German battle fleet, on Fisher, and on the preliminaries leading to the outbreak of the war.

The Jordan anthology [240], dedicated to Marder, contained two pertinent articles: Ruddock Mackay (pp. 32–44) on the Anglo-German naval rivalry and Paul Kennedy (pp. 45–59) with an intriguing comparative essay on Fisher and Tirpitz. Mackay reviewed the historiography, this before Kennedy's book on the subject [250]. Padfield's work [336], which blamed the kaiser, was noted, as were the works of Marder [294, 297] and his own biography of Fisher [287]. From the German perspective, the works of Fritz Fischer [117], Steinberg [437], and Berghahn [32] were cited. Kennedy's piece compared and contrasted the lives and contributions of Fisher and Tirpitz. There were many similarities: both were from the middle class, both arose rapidly and were ennobled, both remained somewhat alienated, both thrived in the materiel atmosphere and were less strategically oriented, both led the preparation of great fleets but neither was in a position to direct them in war, and both remained "on the sidelines." They differed in their social consciousness: Fisher was tolerant and reform-minded while Tirpitz was ultra-patriotic, a social imperialist, and a social Darwinist. Richard Langhorne [262] focused on the years 1912–1914, when there were several opportunities to resolve the conflict short of war.

ADMIRAL SIR JOHN "JACKY" FISHER

For the Royal Navy the dominating personality whom Marder [297], Hough [212], Ollard [523] and others credited with personifying the entire era was "Jacky" Fisher, first sea lord of the Admiralty, 1904–1910 and 1914–1915. Fisher published his own memoirs [118]; there were biographies by Bacon [12], Hough [212], and Mackay [287]; editions of letters and papers by Marder [295] and Kemp [248]; an article by Custer [87]; and Fisher was pervasive, ubiquitous, and the hero in Marder's six volumes [294, 297]. As noted, Kennedy [240, pp. 45–59] and Ollard [523] focus on Fisher.

The best, most balanced, and most comprehensive biography, "warts and all," was by Ruddock Mackay [287], definitely not a panegyric as Marder's [297] and Hough's [212] were. Mackay gave Fisher credit for much, e.g., personnel reforms, improved conditions, and early materiel advances, but Fisher was also blamed for the serious rift in the navy and for the lack of a naval staff; he was accused of abusing Prince Louis of Battenberg and, even worse, Churchill; and Fisher stayed on too long, and then came back again. Like Tirpitz, Fisher became irrelevant and tended toward megalomania in the end. Antony Lambton [261] has a collective biography on the Battenbergs-Mountbattens.

Peter Kemp (pp. 16–31) contributed an article in the Jordan anthology [240] on the regeneration of the Royal Navy after the 1890s from the depths of somnolence, tradition, and ritualistic evolutions through the Fisher reforms, but they were exclusively directed at materiel improvements. Marder depicted a similar scenario in his works [294, 297].

Fisher split the Royal Navy into two factions, supporters called "Fisherites" or "the Fishpond," and opponents of his reforms, centered around Admiral Lord Charles Beresford, a naval commander himself and later member of Parliament. There has been a Duke dissertation-biography on Beresford by Tulenko [470]. THE FLEET THAT JACK BUILT by Sir William S. Jameson [228] actually credited Fisher and eight other leaders, e.g., Beresford, A. K. Wilson, Jellicoe, Beatty, and Lord Keyes, with building the modern Royal Navy. In a specific biography [333] and a general history of guns at sea [337] Peter Padfield credited Sir Percy Scott with initiating the major gunnery improvements during the early decades of the century. As a protégé of Fisher, Scott implemented director firing techniques along with gunnery reform. Scott wrote his memoirs [417].

Mackay also has an article [285] which revised the interpretations about the Fisher-initiated redistribution of the British fleets, 1904–1905. Marder had claimed Fisher was only reacting at that time to the rising German threat; Mackay believed that the Russian and French threats, financial considerations, and crises in the Far East and the Mediterranean were just as influential. John Moore's Columbia dissertation [306] was devoted to determining the various rationales for redistribution of the British fleet and, like Mackay, insisted that there were a variety of reasons including financial and departmental politics, i.e., demands of the foreign office, colonial office, war office, and treasury.

A. M. Gollin [149] has exposed details of Fisher's persistent and effective propaganda efforts with influential journalists, in this case, J. L. Garvin of the OBSERVER. Fisher's often unprofessional machinations with journalists and with leaders of the political opposition, e.g., A. J. Balfour, were significant revelations presented in the Mackay biography [287]. W. Mark Hamilton [176, 177] has produced an informative monograph and article on the whole matter of British navalist propaganda and pressure groups in the decades before World War I. Marder [297] neglected this facet of Fisher's machinations. An Oxford dissertation [492] and article [491], winner of the Julian Corbett Prize, by Rhodri Williams, emphasized the contributions of Balfour to the various Fisher reforms. Richard Ollard [523] has compared Fisher in the World War I era with Admiral A. B. Cunningham of the World War II era. The link was Winston Churchill.

The matters of budgets, finance, money-consciousness, "guns and butter," i.e., in the case of the Liberal government of 1905–1915, the budgeted provisions for DREADNOUGHTS and social reform measures, have increasingly come under scrutiny from recent scholars, notably Sumida [444, 445, 446, 447, 449], Anthony Pollen [358], Charles Fairbanks [514], and Geoffrey Bennett [27]. Marder [294, 297] had comparatively little on these matters; indeed, Sumida and Fairbanks have been quite critical of Marder's research and accounts of them. Geoffrey Bennett [27] noted that Fisher's money-saving endeavors meant less armor protection, especially on his personal favorite design, the battle cruiser, and influenced the decision not to enlarge the width of capital ships. The implication was that wider ships would provide better protection from torpedoes. But it also meant that all existing dry docks and other facilities would have to be enlarged, an

enormously expensive process. The Germans sacrificed and designed wider capital ships; the British did not. These matters are
dealt with from the German perspective in a revisionist essay by
Holger Herwig [518].

Sumida has produced books [449, 451], articles [444, 445], and
papers [446, 450] elaborating on these matters. Fisher's favorite
ship-type was the battle cruiser which, to him, maximized the
advantages of speed, long range, and single-caliber firepower and
at a cheaper price than the DREADNOUGHT battleship; thus, it
was perfect for the needs of "guns and butter." Protection was less
important. The torpedo would not be a threat at long range. Tied
to these characteristics were the needs for effective rangefinding
and fire control. The A. H. Pollen system provided that, but Sir
Reginald Bacon, Jellicoe, and others opposed it, partly because
it was mechanized, and, apparently, partly because Pollen was
a civilian. The inferior system designed by Frederic Dreyer was
adopted. Money was saved on several counts. Sumida concluded
that these deficiencies in design, construction, gunnery, and fire
control, especially in the case of the battle cruisers, caused the
spectacular losses and problems of gunnery at Jutland and other
naval battles during the war. In an essay covering the last century
and a half of technological development in the Royal Navy in the
Haycock anthology [189, pp. 75–92], Sumida observed that the
Admiralty persisted in spending limited funds on the battle fleet,
to the ultimate neglect of submarines and aircraft carriers which
happened to have been the strategic naval forces of the future.

ADMIRAL ALFRED VON TIRPITZ

Tirpitz was a relatively obscure young naval officer serving
in the Far East, and the German navy was a neglected force in
the 1890s, when Kaiser Wilhelm II selected him to build a battle
fleet. Tirpitz was a man of driving and self-serving ambition who
claimed to be influenced by the American naval strategist A. T.
Mahan and the "Blue Water" school of naval warfare involving
battle fleet action. Jutland was reviewed briefly in Tirpitz's memoirs [466]. Tirpitz's papers were also published [467].

Volcker Berghahn [32, 33] and Jonathan Steinberg [434, 435, 436,
437] have been most prolific in assessing the role of Tirpitz in

developing the German battle fleet, its strategy, and its political, social, and naval impact on German society. Berghahn [32, 33] called Tirpitz's naval program "an instrument of distraction and social integration [formulated] to paralyse the pressure for change" [437, p. 29]. It provoked the naval arms race. Holger Herwig [197] described the Tirpitz program not only as an irresponsible luxury but also a deliberate threat. Herwig [518] has raised serious questions about the connections between the DREADNOUGHT revolution, Marder's interpretations [294, 297], and the German reaction. The Tirpitz-Plan for constructing a large battle fleet was based on complex economic, domestic, and foreign motives. Walter Hubatsch [219] has reviewed the Tirpitz era from the German perspective. Gary Weir [487, 488] noted Tirpitz never appreciated the significance or potential of the submarine, seeing it as jeopardizing his battle fleet program. In an unusually critical dissertation Patrick Kelly [247] depicted Tirpitz as a self-serving megalomaniac at the national and the personal levels. In an article [249] Kennedy indicted Tirpitz for persisting with the naval program against the advice of the naval staff and while oblivious to army war planning. A German evaluation was by Michael Salewski [408].

DEVELOPMENT OF THE DREADNOUGHT, BATTLE CRUISERS, AND OTHER WARSHIPS

The ships which fought at Jutland were the culmination of a revolution in naval warship design, construction, propulsion, gunnery, and innovative uses under and above the water. The most extensive general bibliography was by Myron Smith [425]. Marder [294, 297] has much on these matters and a separate article [296].

The earliest standard reference guide on modern warships was the history by William Hovgaard [217], taken from lectures on warship design he presented at the Massachusetts Institute of Technology in 1919. JANE'S [230] and CONWAY'S [77, 78, 79] have published detailed surveys of fighting ships of all of the world's navies, often in the form of annual compilations. They and others have also published similar surveys of individual warships, notably battleships, including the ones which fought on both sides at Jutland: e.g., CONWAY'S ALL THE WORLD'S BATTLESHIPS, 1906 TO THE PRESENT [77], Antony Preston, BATTLESHIPS OF WORLD WAR I [362], and Siegfried Breyer, who has produced two different formats [39, 40] originally in German and translated into English.

The standard technical history and most comprehensive survey of the development of British battleships was by Oscar Parkes [341]. The book was first published in the 1950s, and a new edition came out in 1990. Plans, designs, specifications, and illustrations of all capital ships from HMS WARRIOR to HMS VANGUARD were incorporated. Less revered was a history by Randolph Pears [348]. Barry Coward [83] produced a general history of British capital ships, WARRIOR to VANGUARD.

Two recent works have utilized released Admiralty records with impressive results. Ray A. Burt surveyed British battleships [51, 52], including details on DREADNOUGHT, the INVINCIBLE class of battle cruisers, and others; and a separate three-part article [55] on the ROYAL SOVEREIGN class, begun in 1913 as successor to the QUEEN ELIZABETH class. There were five battleships, all of which fought in World War II, including ROYAL OAK, sunk by U-47 at Scapa Flow in 1939. David K. Brown of the Royal Corps of Naval Constructors published an article on the design and construction of DREADNOUGHT [43] and a book commemorating the 100th anniversary of the Royal Corps of Naval Constructors [42]. A somewhat naive critique of British warship design generally was by G. M. Stephen [440]. Charles Fairbanks [514], Holger Herwig [518], and Jon Sumida [449], all generally at odds with Marder [294, 297], and Archer Jones [237] discussed "the DREADNOUGHT revolution." Richard Hough [215] has produced a history of the post-DREADNOUGHT battleship and an individual "biography" [214] of a unique one, HMS AGINCOURT, which fought at Jutland. IRON DUKE, leading ship of a class of battleships and Jellicoe's flagship at Jutland, has been profiled by Tobias Philbin [354]. WARSPITE, which was damaged and went in circles at a crucial time at Jutland has been chronicled by V. E. Tarrant [528].

Donald Macintyre [283] and Norman Friedman [126] have produced general histories of battleship design and development, the former with emphasis on Great Britain. There was a superficial study by William McMahon [290].

German developments and designs have been analyzed. The first volume of a new history of German warships has appeared, by Eric Groener, covering the period 1815–1945. It was on major surface vessels [159]. There was a general survey by Hans Hansen [517]. Excellent profiles including histories and schematic drawings were forthcoming from Tobias Philbin [355], Paul Schmalenbach [411], and Friedrich Ruge [406].

Sumida [444, 447, 449, 450, 451] has conducted thorough research on the engineering, design, construction, gunnery, and fire control deficiencies, especially of the battle cruisers. Charles Fairbanks has elaborated on these matters in the Cogar anthology [509, pp. 128–38]. V. E. Tarrant [454] singled out the first battle cruiser, INVINCIBLE, for an in-depth study. To him, the lack of armor protection, especially horizontal deck armor, was the most serious flaw. A particularly impressive study was N. John M. Campbell, BATTLECRUISERS [59], which analyzed design and construction features of British and German battle cruisers. The findings related to key factors at issue in the battle of Jutland and others. Campbell's conclusions were as follows: "battle cruiser" rightly defined those capital ships built between 1905–1920 which could make at least four knots faster than contemporary battleships and had less armor protection; the German designs provided more protection and were more successful; the British designs were more vulnerable because of extra weight for the hulls and machinery; contrary to some claims, the Germans had no better anti-flash protection than the British; and the German powder charges and igniters were less volatile than the British. John A. Roberts [385, 386] and Campbell [62, 63] have produced accounts of pertinent classes and individual ships.

Capital ships were not the only warships at Jutland. Cruisers, the "eyes" of the battle fleet, have been reviewed from the years 1880 to 1980 by Antony Preston [363]. There have been two standard comprehensive guides on British destroyers, one by Thomas Manning [292] and the other by Edgar March [293]. Over 1000 vessels were identified with details and illustrations. March has more information on actual operations, including several pages on Jutland (pp. 234–38). Cruisers and destroyers

were also thoroughly covered by Burt [53, 54], Bywater [57], and
Peter Smith [427]. Taprell Dorling, pseud. "Taffrail," has a vivid
and dramatic story of operations of destroyers including actions
at Jutland [511, pp. 149–240].

MATERIEL ADVANCES

The naval "revolution" involved more than warships and warship design. N. John M. Campbell [60] has produced an 18–part
series of articles on modern naval guns. The history of battleship
ordnance from 7–inch guns of the 1860s to the 16–inch guns
of the USS IOWA-class was surveyed by Peter Hodges [204].
Rodrigo Robertson [387] has raised questions about the long-term
effectiveness of the big naval gun. The first volume of a new
study on the history of engineering developments in the Royal
Navy, in this case from 1827 to 1939, has appeared, by Rippon
[383]. It was poorly organized but informative.

Anthony Pollen, son of Arthur Hungerford Pollen, has written
THE GREAT GUNNERY SCANDAL: THE MYSTERY OF JUT-
LAND [358], to vindicate his father in the long conflict with the
Admiralty over a computer-like gun fire control and director
system designed and produced by the elder Pollen, a lawyer,
businessman, engineer, and journalist. The Admiralty was investigating various fire control and rangefinder systems to solve
the gunnery problem under the conditions of battle in the decades
before the war. Admiral Sir Frederic Dreyer ultimately designed
the system adopted by the Admiralty. That system incorporated a
"clock" arrangement, partly Pollen's idea, but the Dreyer system
has been generally condemned as insufficient for the long ranges
and rapidly changing dispositions of twentieth-century capital
ships. Pollen, along with Reginald Hall and Sir Herbert Richmond, had designed a superior system which they claimed could
correctly and rapidly solve long-range problems using an early
computer-like process. Pollen, bitterly disappointed, pursued his
attacks against the Admiralty, influenced the "firing" of Jellicoe
as first sea lord in 1917, and, in the mid-1920s, was awarded
over 25,000 pounds in a judicial suit against the Admiralty for
illegally using his patented inventions. Jon Sumida [444, 447,
449, 451] and the younger Pollen [358] have elaborated on these

matters. The elder Pollen, under his journalist cap, appraised Jutland [525, 526].

Alan Cowpe [84] has a London dissertation on the development of underwater weapons. Edwyn Gray [156], Alan Wolstencroft [499], Eberhard Rossler [398], and Alan Cowpe in the Ranft anthology [375, pp. 23–36] studied the evolution of the torpedo, which was originally invented by an Englishman. Maurice Griffiths [158] covered another innovation, mine warfare.

Vickers, a major arms firm producing warships, submarines, aircraft, and weapons, has been the object of excellent studies: J. D. Scott [416], Clive Trebilcock in a book [469], and a more general study of the armaments industry in an article [468]. The famous ship building region in Scotland, the Clyde, where numerous warships were built, was analyzed by Hugh Peebles [524]. Kay MacLeod in the J. M. Winter anthology [495, pp. 165–203] focused on deficiencies in the British optical industry. Because of "failure of entrepreneurial nerve," Barr and Stroud, producer of rangefinders, sights, and binoculars, remained dependent on German innovations and expertise, e.g., that of Carl Zeiss. An excellent business history of Barr and Stroud, using company archives, has been produced by Michael Moss [310].

There have been several studies of the formal efforts at cooperation between the navy and professional scientists, institutionalized by creation of the Board of Invention and Research in 1915, headed by Fisher. There were serious problems, Fisher's personality among them, and the effort was deemed a failure. Examples of accounts were Hartcup [185], Gusewelle in a dissertation [163] and an article in the Jordan anthology [240, pp. 105–17], and MacLeod [289]. Related studies concerned research associated with underwater warfare, submarines, antisubmarine detection, and underwater weapons such as the torpedo, mine, and depth charge. Hackmann [164, 165] and Brian Head [191] have studied these matters.

EARLY YEARS OF THE WAR

Several minor confrontations in the North Sea between parts of the battle fleets occurred during the early years, e.g., Heligoland Bight in 1914 and Dogger Bank in 1915. James Goldrick [147] has provided a comprehensive and informative survey of these early naval operations in the North Sea, the period of "the true beginning of modern naval warfare," partly because, for the first time, it was warfare in three dimensions; undersea, surface, and air. Communication was enhanced by the wireless, torpedo and mine warfare were new, and surface actions involved longer ranges and faster speeds. The Germans had not anticipated the "far blockade" strategy and suffered from a flawed command structure. Goldrick also introduced a reprinting of Filson Young's WITH THE BATTLE CRUISERS [505], about the early years of the war in the North Sea. The American title was WITH BEATTY IN THE NORTH SEA.

Chapter 3

THE BATTLE

PREPARATION AND PRELIMINARIES

The matters of naval intelligence and conveying known and vital intelligence information to the proper commanders, Admirals Beatty and Jellicoe, has been a bone of contention. The view seems to be that intelligence operatives in Room 40, the Admiralty intelligence center at Whitehall, knew precisely that Admiral Scheer had transferred his radio call ashore early on 31 May, an indication that he was under way. The Admiralty operations officer, Sir Henry F. "Dummy" Oliver, asked Room 40 if Scheer's radio call was under way and Room 40 rightly answered that it was not. Oliver and the Admiralty did not ask more productive questions and simply assumed Scheer was still in port on the morning of 31 May. Jellicoe and Beatty were so informed. That caused them to act in a different manner than they would have had they known otherwise. Indeed, Beatty was assured Scheer was in port only a short time before Hipper and the rest of the High Seas Fleet were actually sighted well out in the North Sea. Sir William James [227] wrote a biography of Oliver and Oliver's papers were collected [330].

Thus, for this and other reasons, the Admiralty has been seriously criticized for incompetence in sufficiently investigating the actual disposition of the High Seas Fleet and for failure to provide Jellicoe with adequate and correct information before and during the battle.

This may be the proper place for an observation about navigation and dead reckoning by the Grand Fleet. From reconstruction later it has been determined that none of the ships of the Grand Fleet had accurate navigational information about individual locations during the battle; errors were as great as 11 miles in some exaggerated cases. After the battle Oswald Frewen initiated an effort which located the wreck of HMS INVINCIBLE, and that provided a precise location from which a reconstruction of tracks could be formulated. During the battle the fleet was relying exclusively on dead reckoning partly because of the haze which made celestial navigation difficult if not impossible. Apparently, alternative methods of navigation were available but not utilized. The cumulative effects were such that on those rare occasions when reports were made of sightings of the enemy and for other reasons, no one knew where they were and some of the reports simply added to the overall confusion. Jellicoe, whose own position was in error, received a few, but wildly erratic, reports of positions of other forces and of the enemy. It was under such circumstances that Jellicoe had to make the decision of when and where to deploy the Grand Fleet. These issues were delineated in a 1927 article by F. P. Evans [110]. It was like blind man's bluff, Evans concluded.

The Germans suffered from similar problems; the cumbersome command structure and ineffective leadership on the part of Scheer have been cited most often. The weather created obstacles as well. Elaborate plans to use zeppelins for reconnaissance had to be cancelled due to the haze.

PHASES OF THE BATTLE

The initial sightings of the scouting cruisers of the opposing fleets occurred at about 2:30 PM on 31 May 1916. At that time Admiral Hipper and his force of battle cruisers were out ahead of Scheer and the High Seas Fleet, headed generally north. Beatty and his force came in from the west with Jellicoe and the Grand Fleet to the north.

Before Marder's volume III [297], the best book on the tactical aspects of the battle on the part of the Germans and British was that of H. H. Frost [127], an American naval officer who researched and interviewed in Great Britain and Germany. There was a German translation [129]. He assessed the tactical capabilities of the four commanders: Hipper gave by far the best performance; Scheer made many errors but should be credited with the successful escape; Jellicoe conducted his fleet ably but with an erroneous conception of naval warfare, and Beatty made numerous errors and had no tactical skill. Frost, a destroyerman himself, rated the British destroyer operations as unsatisfactory. Charles Gill [145] has conducted a study of the tactics of the battle.

PHASE I: "RUN TO THE SOUTH," c. 2:30 to 5:00 PM

Admiral Sir William Goodenough, commander of the Second Light Cruiser squadron, initially discovered the presence of the High Seas Fleet during the Run to the South and immediately reported to the commander-in-chief. This was one of the rare reports received by Jellicoe. Goodenough [151] published his memoirs and gave an interview to the BBC [150].

Beatty was commander of the Battle Cruiser force which, on the day of Jutland, included six battle cruisers and the four new battleships of the QUEEN ELIZABETH class of the Fifth Battle Squadron under Admiral Sir Hugh Evan-Thomas. Once Hipper was sighted, the battle of Jutland opened with Beatty chasing Hipper to the south. This was the point at which one of the most persistent controversial issues originated. The Fifth Battle Squadron was disposed in a direction away from the enemy; serious confusion and delays eventuated over signals from Beatty's flagship, HMS LION, to Evan-Thomas concerning expeditious engagement; the Fifth Battle Squadron missed 20 minutes of the most crucial part of this phase of the battle; and when finally engaged, the squadron tactically conducted a turn which meant each ship moved through the same point, effectively providing a permanent aiming spot for enemy guns. Beatty and his staff have been faulted in this and in earlier battles for incompetence, a communications imbroglio, perpetuating confusion, and failure to convey vital information to Jellicoe. Perhaps more seriously, criticism for the failure to concentrate forces for battle has been leveled at Beatty.

Evan-Thomas came under much criticism for these events. In an article in 1935 Craig Waller [481] presented an apology for Evan-Thomas and the Fifth Battle Squadron. Problems were due to lapses in communication and poor direction from Beatty's flagship. F. P. Evans [110] focused on this phase and reviewed all of the communications debacle, miscalculations, and faulty tactics, blaming Beatty for being ineffective and incompetent, and comparing this escapade to the Charge of the Light Brigade. Fisher dubbed Beatty "Balaklava Beatty"!

Campbell [61] determined that during this phase the British suffered 62 hits and the Germans 36 hits. This definitive analysis was at odds with outrageous claims made later by Admiral Lord Alfred Chatfield, Beatty's flag captain, and other pro-Beatty adherents, that the British battle cruiser gunnery was very effective at this time but defective fuse design meant numerous duds. HMS INDEFATIGABLE and QUEEN MARY, battle cruisers of Beatty's force, were blown up during this phase.

PHASE II: "RUN TO THE NORTH," c. 5:00 to 6:00 PM

Upon sighting the entire High Seas Fleet, Beatty's force immediately reversed course so as to lead the German force to the north toward the Grand Fleet. In the Run to the North, Beatty has been faulted for losing touch with the enemy, and, upon joining up with the Grand Fleet, being unable to report his or the enemy's positions. He then proposed, and proceeded to carry out, a maneuver which caused massive confusion and fouled the gunnery of the Grand Fleet for several vital minutes: a complicated exercise to place his entire force in the van of the Grand Fleet. Evan-Thomas, following with the Fifth Battle Squadron, perceived the potential disruption and fell in astern of the Grand Fleet.

PHASE III: MAIN BATTLE FLEET
CONFRONTATION, c. 6:00 to 9:00 PM

Among the controversial issues associated with this phase of the battle, two stand out when the two main battle fleets confronted each other, twice. The first was the question of the deployment of the Grand Fleet, i.e., how, when, and where to shift the fleet from a cruising formation in columns to a single line ahead so that the maximum fire power could be concentrated on the enemy. Much debate ensued after the battle, and for decades thereafter, about the time and the direction of the deployment. The decision about when and in what direction to deploy the fleet was made by Jellicoe; it was perhaps the most important decision of his entire life. At a time when the information he had and was receiving was inadequate and confused—remember that the dead reckoning tracks were in error by as much as eleven nautical miles, that few of the pertinent commanders were feeding him information at all, and the meager amount of information he was receiving was wrong and confusing—Jellicoe opted to deploy to port or in an eastward direction. The deployment actually put the Grand Fleet in a position so that the "T" of the High Seas Fleet to the south was being crossed. The same deployment was resumed after the "turn away" so that the "T" of the High Seas Fleet was crossed a second time.

The second crucial issue during the main battle fleet confrontation phase was Jellicoe's decision to turn away from any torpedo attack. This he did at Jutland, which meant that the Grand Fleet almost immediately lost contact with the High Seas Fleet and battle was disengaged. He had always said that he would turn away, because that configuration and direction meant the torpedoes were least likely to hit their targets. Jellicoe has been accused of cowardliness, unimaginativeness, and purposely breaking off battle at the very time when the Grand Fleet was enjoying maximum advantage. He has also been praised for not unduly jeopardizing the fleet at an extremely vulnerable time. The torpedo was greatly feared. Whether that was justified or not was immaterial.

In an essay in volume I of Allan Millett, MILITARY EFFECTIVENESS [303, pp. 31-79], Paul Kennedy, evaluating the military effectiveness of the Royal Navy in World War I, determined that the British strategy in the North Sea was essentially correct, and noted that Jellicoe, and even more so, Beatty, after him as commander of the Grand Fleet, correctly acted with much caution because there was no need for unnecessary risks, and that Jellicoe's turn away tactic was inglorious, but sensible.

Another common complaint against Jellicoe was his excessive caution and failure to aggressively engage the enemy at every opportunity. Again, Jellicoe had answered such critics before the battle. He was fully aware that, as Churchill put it, he was the only man who could lose the war in an afternoon, i.e., the danger existed that dozens of capital ships could be sunk in a short time, precisely the objective of the Germans. If that did happen to the British, there was no second or third line of defense. All would be lost and humiliating surrender must inevitably follow. So, for Jellicoe, the safe decision was extreme caution. Ironically, it was Churchill [73] who attacked Jellicoe's cautious policies most critically.

Campbell [61] determined that during this phase the British suffered 23 hits, a total of 122 for the battle, while the Germans suffered 68 hits, a total of 123 for the battle. The British fired a total of 4480 shots from guns of all calibers, with 122 hits or a percentage of hits of 2.75; the Germans fired 3597 shots, with 123 hits or a percentage of hits of 3.39.

PHASE IV: NIGHT ACTION, FROM ABOUT 9:00 PM, 31 MAY TO ABOUT NOON, 1 JUNE

Massive confusion ensued during this phase. Scheer's intention was to escape in the most expeditious way and return to the safety of his base. Jellicoe intended to cut off that escape and to resume the main fleet action early the next morning. The persistent problems of the British, e.g., communications, the failure to report sightings, and confusion over location, continued to plague their operations. These were exaggerated by the poor performance of the British searchlights and night operations, for which there had previously been little or no practice. The Germans seemed to have suffered less from these problems and certainly performed better in the matter of searchlight use and night fighting tactics.

There were some violent but isolated skirmishes, many involving destroyers, during the evening. The German fleet somehow passed through the Grand Fleet's track that evening and managed to reach the announced rendezvous prior to entering port the next morning. Room 40 did pick up and decipher pertinent messages from Scheer about his plans and anticipated locations, but, again, these vital and informative messages were not forwarded to Jellicoe. It was thus that the battle of Jutland came to an end.

Chapter 4

THE ASSESSMENT

TABLE OF BATTLE STATISTICS

British total forces—Grand Fleet, Jellicoe, commander:

- 28 battleships (4 under Beatty)
- 9 battle cruisers (6 under Beatty)
- 34 cruisers
- 80 destroyers

British losses:

- 3 battle cruisers
- 3 cruisers
- 8 destroyers
- lost 111,980 tons of ships
- 6945 casualties
- 6094 killed

On 1 June, 28 capital ships of the Grand Fleet were ready for operations.

German total forces—High Seas Fleet, Scheer, commander:

- 16 battleships
- 6 pre-DREADNOUGHTS
- 5 battle cruisers (5 under Hipper)
- 11 cruisers
- 63 destroyers

German losses:

- 2 battleships
- 4 cruisers
- 5 destroyers
- lost 62,233 tons of ships
- 3058 casualties
- 2551 killed

On 1 June, 10 capital ships of the High Seas Fleet were ready for action.

It should therefore be observed that on 1 June 1916 the Grand Fleet was fully operational and ready for battle, not counting the relatively few ships seriously damaged. By contrast, the High Seas Fleet was in no condition to fight and would not be for several months.

THE BATTLE OF JUTLAND OR THE BATTLE OFF THE SKAGERRAK

Marder [297], of course, has the most comprehensive account of all aspects of the battle. Volume III was entitled JUTLAND AND AFTER, MAY 1916–DECEMBER 1916, and was dedicated "To the memory of two distinguished Admirals, upholders of a proud tradition: Lords Jellicoe and Beatty." Attached in a packet in the back were 14 detailed charts of the battle formulated by the former director of the Tactical School of the Royal Navy,

Captain John Creswell. Marder explained that one aspect of the revised edition incorporated suggestions and reported research in correspondence with an impressive list of experts, including Sir William James, B. B. Schofield, Chalmers, Kemp, Kennedy, Schurman, Campbell, Friedrich Stahl, and Friedrich Ruge, the latter two prominent German scholars. A. D. Lutzow [279] produced a survey of the early German naval operations, including Jutland, sponsored by MARINEARCHIV, the naval archives.

In the definitive study of the gunnery action of the battle, Campbell [61] made the following conclusions: the British fire-control, director control, and Dreyer firing tables were superior—a conclusion definitely at odds with traditional interpretations; German stereoscopic rangefinders were superior; British armor-piercing shells performed very poorly: only 3 of 15 hits of heavy shells functioned as designed; the most serious problems of the British concerned the make-up and storage of powder and the design of the magazines; German flash protection remained inferior to the British—another conclusion at odds; losses of the three British battle cruisers would not have been prevented with more armor protection; the 200 torpedoes fired at Jutland scored only 8 or 9 hits, mostly by British torpedoes; and underwater protection was inferior for both fleets, e.g., LUTZOW sank because of flooding despite the much-praised subdivision arrangements on the German ships. Sumida [449] effectively supplements our knowledge on these matters.

Overall, as Bryan Ranft pointed out in the Turner anthology [472, pp. 53–69], Jutland, indeed the naval war in full, represented paradox and disappointment. The Grand Fleet failed to gain a decisive victory, yet the Royal Navy protected Britain and the empire and denied the seas to the enemy. Corbett's essentials had been fulfilled. Trevor Wilson, in the MYRIAD FACES OF WAR [494], assessed the battle from the British perspective and concluded it was not a great naval battle but a "non-battle" and that no startling changes ensued (pp. 298–300).

The three–volume anthology of Allan Millett, MILITARY EFFECTIVENESS, assessed that feature in World War I, the interwar period, in World War II; Paul Kennedy contributed the final summary essay on World War I [303, pp. 329–50] and determined that there was general military incompetence by the generals and the admirals. The main fleet operations, Dogger Bank and Jutland, were chance encounters. Operational expertise had not caught up with the new technology, Kennedy concluded.

Russell Grenfell [157] clarified the role of the older armored cruiser at Jutland. HMS DEFENCE blew up and WARRIOR was heavily damaged. Criticisms were raised that they and other obsolete warships were in the wrong place and their commanders were guilty of "reckless impetuosity" and obstructing operations of the capital ships. A novel by A. E. Langsford [521] included an incident associated with the loss of WARRIOR.

SUBMARINE AND AIR WARFARE

For a variety of reasons the underwater and the air dimensions of warfare from the German and British sides were extremely limited at Jutland, but the potential was there for both and there had been much anticipation and preparation to use both. Winston Churchill was an early air enthusiast. Jellicoe had actually qualified as an aviator and Beatty supported air tactics. Submarines, airships, seaplane tenders, and airplanes were available for reconnaissance and other operations at the time of the battle. The Germans had zeppelins in place and planned to use them as an integral part of their forces at Jutland, but the weather precluded such operations. Some zeppelins went aloft that day. The Germans also had sent U-boats out days before the sortie with the objective of attacking the ships of the Grand Fleet as they departed from their bases. A British seaplane "carrier" was attached to Beatty's force. A British aircraft was aloft and reported targets during the battle. Because of mechanical problems, confusion, and mismanagement of communications, air power played no role for the British.

Myron Smith has produced a bibliography and chronology on World War I in the air [426]. The earliest developments in aviation and precursors of the aircraft carrier, all the way back to the 1780s!, e.g., balloons, kites, and airships, have been imaginatively and thoroughly reviewed by R. D. Layman [263, 264]. A. M. Gollin in THE IMPACT OF AIR POWER [148] has comprehensively and delightfully reviewed all aspects of the original efforts of the British in reaction to this new dimension of warfare. A general history of naval aviation has been produced by a great destroyer commander during World War II, Donald Macintyre [284]. Desmond Young described the career of an early naval aviator, F. J. Rutland, in the context of reviewing early developments, RUTLAND OF JUTLAND [504]. HMS ENGADINE was a seaplane tender and was located in the North Sea. On 31 May 1916, Rutland flew his seaplane on a reconnaissance mission, sighted a force of German cruisers and destroyers, and transmitted three position reports by radio. This was the first effort ever of aircraft involvement in a naval battle. Unfortunately, the radio reports were not picked up. A dissertation by Lewis Pulsipher [368] and an article by Joseph Palmer [340] lamented the neglect of the air service. There were accounts by Aaron Norman [322], J. M. Bruce [46, 47], and an oral history by Peter Liddle [272].

The zeppelin program of Germany has been reviewed by Raymond Rimell [382] and Douglas Robinson [389]. Robinson also has the best scholarly study of the history of airships [388]. Robin Higham, in a book [199] and an article in the Jordan anthology [240, pp. 90–104], has studied the failed British efforts to develop a rigid airship program.

Eberhard Rossler [399] has one of the best surveys of German submarine development. He noted U-boats were not successful at Jutland (p. 66). British submarine activities at Jutland have not been recounted separately.

DISPOSITIONS OF THE BATTLE FLEETS

After the battle both fleets returned to their bases where repairs and resupplying were expedited. The Germans had suffered significantly more repairable damage and that process required some weeks and extensive resources. The Grand Fleet was fully operational and ready for further operations within hours. David Woodward has compiled a general reference guide on the circumstances of all capital ship losses [501]. There was also an official compilation of British ship losses [41].

The design, construction, and engineering "lessons" from Jutland were incorporated into post-war British-built capital ships. N. John M. Campbell [63] has an informative four-part article on the "Cherry-tree" class of ships, which were redesigned and "cut-down" due to the provisions of the Washington Naval Conference treaty on naval arms limitation. Originally there were to be four "G-3s," each with nine 18–inch guns and a speed of 23 knots, but only HMS HOOD was completed. Obviously "all" of the lessons were not learned because HOOD blew up in a famous confrontation with the German warships BISMARCK and PRINZ EUGENE early in World War II.

The disposition of the High Seas Fleet has been of interest to historians. Effectively, it never came out again in search of battle. Rebellion, degeneration, demoralization, and mutiny ensued. There were rumors and apparent plans for some last sortie/suicide mission in the weeks before the war ended. Hipper, who became commander later, has been linked to that proposed operation. The mutiny precluded that possibility. At the armistice the Allied authorities provided that the entire fleet with the necessary personnel, officers and sailors, be interned—techni-cally, there was no formal surrender. The former High Seas Fleet was escorted under armed guard to the large harbor north of Scotland, Scapa Flow, Orkney Islands, where the Grand Fleet also was based. Daniel Horn [209, 211] was the best authority on the German naval mutinies; David Woodward, the BBC journalist, has an account [500]. An oral history of British operatives and life at Scapa Flow has been produced by Malcolm Brown [44].

At Scapa Flow on 21 June, seven days before the signing of the Treaty of Versailles in Paris in 1919, by secret coordination, the entire fleet was scuttled on signal at the same time. It was speculated that an Allied ultimatum about resumption of the war affected the local German commander's decision. That commander, Ludwig von Reuter, has published his recollections [380]. Those ships which sank were 15 of 16 capital ships, 5 of 8 cruisers, and 32 of 50 destroyers. All 1820 officers and men then became prisoners of war; two officers and six men were killed in the scuttling operation.

There were a number of accounts: Dan Van der Vat [476], who reviewed the history of the High Seas Fleet from beginning (c. 1898) to end; Ludwig Freiwald of NASSAU [120] recalled the last days; Friedrich Ruge, a participant, wrote a book [404] and article [405]; Gerald Bowman [36] told the story of Ernest Frank

Guelph Cox, an engineer, who purchased the rights to salvage the
entire fleet, an eight-year operation; and S. C. George, JUTLAND
TO JUNKYARD [135], and David Ferguson, THE WRECKS OF
SCAPA FLOW [115], reviewed the ultimate disposition of each
individual ship.

Chapter 5

VARIOUS ACCOUNTS AND
THE CONTROVERSY

INTRODUCTION

Marder's volume V of FROM DREADNOUGHT [297] contained
one of the best bibliographies of the battle of Jutland and the
subsequent controversy. In many respects that dispute presented
an outstanding case study and lesson in historiography. Bibliographical information on Jutland can also be found in the second
edition (1978) of volume III [297].

Looking at the process of the development of public reaction
and feelings it has become clear that the following sequence
occurred: Beatty was initially seen by virtually all to be the great,
dashing, and aggressive hero of the battle—and he was favored in
the official reward system. A myth was created. In the meantime
Jellicoe, perceived as overly cautious and detached from events,
was blamed for failure to win a decisive victory. But, over several
decades, and especially after more details of the battle became
known to the public, Jellicoe was seen as the sagacious and
brilliant tactician, certainly the victim of gross neglect by the
Admiralty and ill-served by subordinates, while Beatty was
exposed as incompetent, blundering, and oblivious of the respon-
sibilities of leadership. Official rewards were ultimately equal-
ized. The traditional method of promulgating announcements
of all honors, promotions, citations of extraordinary action, and

awards was in the LONDON GAZETTE, in this case the third supplement of December 1916 [277].

THE COMMUNIQUÉS

The German announcement to the public of the results of the battle came out first, within hours after the High Seas Fleet returned to base. It proclaimed a great victory. Part of the reason for the magnitude and persistence of the Jutland controversy later was the fact that this announcement turned out to be a propaganda coup for Germany and nothing the British could do, then or later, seemed to have been able to change that initial perception.

The author of the demoralizing British communiqué, which was the original document launching the British controversy, was Arthur James Balfour, first lord at the time of Jutland and a former prime minister. There were, in fact, important extenuating circumstances for the timing and information conveyed in the communiqué, but they have seemed to be irrelevant and certainly not persuasive to critics. Balfour's assessment has been described as endorsing the German claim of victory and disseminating a false impression of disaster. Balfour has been the subject of good biographies: Ruddock Mackay [286], Lord Egremont [107], Kenneth Young [506], and the older authorized one by Blanche Dugdale [100]. John Buchan [49, p. 255] described the British communiqué as having "a candour which may have been undiplomatic."

Stuart Sillars [422] analyzed the use of art and propaganda in warfare, citing British incidents associated with Jutland as examples. The communiqué reflected uncertainty of purpose and naivete in understanding the public and produced some unfortunate effects. Even the supplementary note written by Winston Churchill "backfired," another demonstration of the lack of awareness of the public mood, Sillars concluded.

THE ACCOUNTS BEGIN

Within weeks of the battle John Leyland [270] had edited a 32–page SOUVENIR OF THE GREAT NAVAL BATTLE AND ROLL OF HONOUR, sponsored by United Newspapers. It opened with a full-page portrait of Beatty, and contained an article about Jellicoe, "Britain's Future Nelson"; one on Beatty, "The Spirit of Sea Power Incarnate"; and some accounts of the battle, though not informative in detail.

The earliest authorized publication about the battle to come from the British was a 100-page pamphlet edited by C. Sanford Terry, THE BATTLE OF JUTLAND BANK [460], consisting of an introductory note (pp. 5–22), reports from Jellicoe and Beatty (pp. 23–93), and concluding with an index of participating ships, persons, and organizations.

The HARPER RECORD [182] was completed in October 1919 by a committee of five experts headed by Commander J.E.T. Harper, who was a navigation expert and not a participant at Jutland. Harper claimed it was "simply a plain, straightforward narrative." The original report of the committee was never published. Mutilation, "tortuous manoeuvers and official prevarications" followed, and the residue was published in 1927. Winton [496] claimed it was "greeted with a great roar of uninterest" (p. 294). Harper's explanation of these machinations was published in Patterson's edition of Jellicoe's papers, appendix to volume II [345].

Harper was involved directly in two subsequent publications, THE TRUTH ABOUT JUTLAND, which appeared in 1927 [184], and, with Langhorne Gibson [138], THE RIDDLE OF JUTLAND, published in 1934. TRUTH championed Jellicoe but was generally restrained on Beatty. RIDDLE purported to be an unbiased, accurate, and clear account. In fact, it was overdramatized and outrageous in its claims of solving all of the mysteries. Jellicoe's deployment order was "the inspiration of genius," and the battle fleet phase was "under the master hand of the British Navy's greatest strategist and tactician." It presented the extenuating circumstances bearing on Balfour's formulation and release of the Admiralty communiqué. Gibson and Harper resented the fact that Beatty received a larger gratuity (100,000 and 50,000 pounds, respectively) and a higher peerage than did Jellicoe initially.

The "public" cried for some details and analysis of the battle. The authorities kept promising that such would be forthcoming momentarily. The promised HARPER RECORD [182], and the NAVAL STAFF APPRECIATION [316] were initially suppressed.

Although Jellicoe had been unceremoniously "fired" as first sea lord in December 1917, after the war he was ceremoniously sent off on a highly publicized, prestigious tour of the Dominions. It was after this mission that Jellicoe was raised to the title of Earl Jellicoe of Scapa. The mission delayed completion of his memoirs. Jellicoe published THE GRAND FLEET in 1919 [233], a summary of the activities and actions of the British force while Jellicoe was commander, and included charts and diagrams. About one-fourth was devoted to Jutland and his "Reflections." He followed this the next year with THE CRISIS OF THE NAVAL WAR [232], but that dealt exclusively with the German U-boat campaign, "the gravest peril which ever threatened the population of this country" (p. vii). Jellicoe prepared a second, revised, and updated edition of THE GRAND FLEET, but his publisher was sceptical of the demand and did not publish it. The Jellicoe "Autobiography" [231] was deposited with the Jellicoe papers at the British Library. Roskill wrote an article [393] on Jellicoe's dismissal.

Arthur H. Pollen, this time in the stance of journalist—he was a business man and brilliant engineer who had designed a computer-like fire control system—published THE BRITISH NAVY IN BATTLE [359], a conventional version of several battles including Jutland.

In 1920 the Lloyd George government published a Blue Book, OFFICIAL DISPATCHES [19], a heterogeneous collection of documents, messages, and reports with no commentary or analysis.

In the meantime, Carlyon Bellairs, commander, RN, published THE BATTLE OF JUTLAND: THE SOWING AND THE REAPING [26] in 1920. One of the earliest public accounts, this was a pro-Beatty encomium with shrill, accusatory language. The truth was being withheld, in what he called "the hush-hush policy," Balfour had refused to assemble a court-martial to allocate blame, and information was being suppressed. Chapter titles exposed the tenor: "Beatty Delivers the High Seas Fleet to His Chief," "The Theory of Deployment," and "Eleven Destroyers Dismiss 27 Battleships."

Sir Reginald Bacon raised the heat and emotion of the controversy to new heights with THE JUTLAND SCANDAL, published in 1924 [11], an early pro-Jellicoe piece by a fierce partisan. Bacon explained that the "scandal" was a "smoke screen" being put up by the current authorities and the press to prevent the public from learning the truth about the battle. The ADMIRALTY NARRATIVE [2] was blatantly pro-Beatty, focusing on the battle cruiser action. Key episodes were glossed over. The HARPER RECORD [182] and NAVAL OPERATIONS, the official history [80], had been suppressed and there was no one who would present the facts as promised by the government and the Admiralty immediately after the battle and the war. An interview with Admiral Scheer published in the DAILY EXPRESS and Filson Young's article in the SUNDAY EXPRESS (10 August 1924) both ignorantly condemned Jellicoe, and Bacon had written both papers with his objections. Scheer claimed Jellicoe had thrown away the opportunity to annihilate the High Seas Fleet. Bacon actually reproduced the Filson Young article (pp. 110–26) followed by a point-by-point refutation. Young immediately went to court and caused THE JUTLAND SCANDAL to be withdrawn because of copyright infringement. Bacon indicted Beatty for, among other things, being responsible for the debacle around the Fifth Battle Squadron in Phase I and with failure to keep Jellicoe informed with vital information. Goodenough [151], one of the few commanders at Jutland whose reputation then and later was enhanced, denounced Harper [184] and Bacon [11] for being too biased.

VARIOUS STUDIES AND INVESTIGATIONS

Beatty's supporters had the Dewar brothers, A. C. and K.G.B., prepare the NAVAL STAFF APPRECIATION [316], and it was ready in August 1921. However, an immediate outcry arose and all copies were ordered to be withdrawn. Jellicoe was among those deploring the selection of these inexperienced and unknown officers.

The ADMIRALTY NARRATIVE [2], published in 1924, was essentially the NAVAL STAFF APPRECIATION [316] without the judgments and criticisms. Roskill [390, p. 333] declared it "devenomized." Although all copies of the NAVAL STAFF APPRECIATION were supposed to be burned, several did survive. Goodenough [151] denounced its partiality.

An early German critique of the war including an account

of Skagerrak, the German name of the battle, and a synopsis of Scheer and Hipper was by Lothar Persius [351], a German naval captain. Admiral Reinhard Scheer wrote his memoirs, which have been translated [410], and if one wades through the ultra-patriotic rhetoric, one can be adequately informed of the German perspective on Jutland.

Otto Groos [160] was the editor of the official German naval history of the war, DER KRIEG SUR SEE, in six volumes. An English translation was published in 1926. The Germans insisted Jutland was their victory but they did admit suffering heavy damage. Their version was favorable to Jellicoe who was praised repeatedly, e.g., for his method of deployment. Groos insisted that the ADMIRALTY NARRATIVE [2] was inaccurate in several essential details, reaffirming Jellicoe's complaints.

Meantime the Committee of Imperial Defence had created a naval historical section and Julian Corbett was engaged to write the official naval history of the war. In the early 1920s the Admiralty interrogated Corbett relentlessly, some claimed to an excessive degree verging on censorship. The first two volumes came out on schedule despite Churchill's rigorous interference. Corbett's NAVAL OPERATIONS, volume III [80], was published shortly after Corbett's death in 1922, and with a strong disclaimer by the Admiralty. Notwithstanding the Admiralty disclaimer, Corbett was seriously limited because he was not permitted to include any hint of intelligence operations or activities of the Admiralty. Volume III of Corbett's NAVAL OPERATIONS [80] was revised in 1940. Only then was it revealed that the Admiralty had seriously blundered in matters of communications, staff work, conveying intelligence and other vital information to the commander, and general oversight. Much later the facts of the achievements of Room 40 and various intelligence coups were revealed. Robin Higham [202] has edited the standard, indeed the only, comprehensive survey of official histories.

In a review in JRUSI, John Leighton [266] praised Corbett's history of Jutland in NAVAL OPERATIONS [80]. Recalling several "previous failures to prepare authentic and complete accounts," Leighton was pleased finally to receive "the facts" which spoke for themselves. Clearly, the strategic situation had not been changed by the battle.

Winston Churchill had already made a significant literary reputation as a journalist and, for example, was called in to write the supplementary communiqué after Jutland. Churchill began THE WORLD CRISIS [73], what would eventually become a six–volume survey of the war and its aftermath. Churchill's third volume of THE WORLD CRISIS [73], including his interpretation of Jutland, was published in 1927. He was unusually critical of Jellicoe, notably his excessive caution not only at Jutland but throughout his tenure as commander. Churchill obviously relied on the version in the condemned NAVAL STAFF APPRECIATION. Jellicoe was extremely upset by this attack. Bacon and others [14] immediately wrote a full-fledged critique of Churchill's WORLD CRISIS [73].

A more professional and systematic assessment and critique of Churchill's WORLD CRISIS was formulated by Robin Prior [366]. Prior concluded that Churchill was often inaccurate and self-serving, e.g., concerning the Dardanelles campaign, but the compassion and literary style offset some deficiencies.

C.R.M.F. Cruttwell's section on Jutland in his general history of the war [85], published in 1935 and just reprinted in 1990, provoked reaction, especially from the pro-Beatty contingent. Cruttwell linked the failure at Jutland and the outbreak of the Russian Revolution! Trevor Wilson [494, p. 297] denounced such outrageous claims by Cruttwell and by Hough [213] as "jingo history" in its most unreflective form.

K.G.B. Dewar published his memoirs [94] in 1939, continuing as an apologist for Beatty. He called the HARPER RECORD [182] "no more than a bald chronological account of the movements" (p. 265), and claimed Beatty in no way interfered with Corbett's NAVAL OPERATIONS [80].

Frederic C. Dreyer [98], Jellicoe's flag captain, published his memoirs in 1955. He focused on Beatty's communications problems with the Fifth Battle Squadron during the first phase, faulting Beatty for failure to concentrate his forces before proceeding into battle. He also attacked Churchill's version [73].

Chatfield, Beatty's flag captain, to whom he made the famous "our bloody ships" assessment, wrote his autobiography [72]. Chatfield played up the battle cruiser action in phase I and consistently denounced the British projectiles as defective.

Rev. John Pastfield, sometime lecturer at the naval war college, in NEW LIGHT ON JUTLAND, published in 1933 [342], concentrated on technical aspects in a pro-Beatty booklet. He attributed loss of the three battle cruisers to "cordite danger."

The definitive biography of Admiral von Hipper has recently been published by Tobias Philbin [352]. Subtitled "The Inconvenient Hero," the book depicts Hipper as a nineteenth-century romantic too late for his time and somewhat alienated from the establishment—Tirpitz disliked him and Scheer envied him. This has been the only professional biography of one of the key German commanders. It was originally from a London dissertation [353] and was published in the Netherlands. Hipper has been universally praised as a brilliant tactician at Jutland, e.g., by Marder [297], Frost [127], Scheer [410], Raeder [369], Doenitz [95], Ruge [404], Bennett [27], and Herwig [197], while Horn [209] has been a critic.

Later grand admirals of the revived German navy under Hitler recalled events of World War I. Erich Raeder [369] devoted several pages to Jutland (pp. 64–78) including the Jellicoe-Beatty controversy and praise for the Groos [160] and Frost [127] accounts. Doenitz's memoirs [95] and a biography by Peter Padfield [335] contained little about the battle although he was a British prisoner at the end of the war, as was a post–World War II commander, Friedrich Ruge [404]. There was a history of the war at sea by Wilhelm Wolfslalt [498].

The destroyer OBDURATE was screening Beatty's force and was in the middle of the hottest action. Aboard was H.P.K. Oram [331], who described seeing LION hit and INDEFATIGABLE and QUEEN MARY blow up. He noted that the destroyers were "lost" during most of the battle because of errors of navigation.

Victor Hayward was an enlisted man aboard TIGER, a battle cruiser at Jutland, who wrote his memoirs [190]. Other similar oral histories have appeared. John Irving was a midshipman at Jutland who later wrote the well-informed SMOKE SCREEN OF JUTLAND [225]. Jellicoe could do no wrong—wise, shrewd, a Nelson—and Beatty only blundered and precipitated a chain of misadventures. Georg von Hase [186], gunnery officer of DERFFLINGER, recounted his experiences of the war beginning with the famous Kiel Week of 1914 and concluding with bitter criticism against the peace treaty. It was translated as KIEL AND JUTLAND. Daniel Horn [210] has edited recollections from Seaman Stumpf of the German navy.

Fawcett and Hooper [114] have edited collective oral histories of 45 officers and men of the British fleet at Jutland. German and British eyewitness accounts of all phases of the battle have been effectively collected by Stuart Legg [265], who had previously edited a similar approach to the battle of Trafalgar of 1805. Peter Liddle, noted archivist and collector of oral histories, photographs, and memorabilia of World War I at Sunderland Polytechnic, included Jutland in his THE SAILOR'S WAR [273]. Letters and diaries of individuals of the Royal Marines, some at Jutland, have been presented by S. M. Holloway [206]. Her account included "mud" and "blue" marines.

Earl Mountbatten [311] wrote a short memoir of his being assigned to LION, Beatty's flagship, a short time after the battle. He credited the failure at Jutland to British design and ordnance problems and the lack of a naval staff.

OTHER PUBLISHED ASSESSMENTS

N. John M. Campbell, the expert metallurgist, has conducted an extensive analysis [61] using German and British sources of all of the ordnance expended by all caliber guns of both sides, the hits which occurred, the damage inflicted, and the damage control which resulted. Significant findings and conclusions of Campbell are summarized throughout this narrative.

Geoffrey Bennett's [27, 28] and Donald Macintyre's [282] were straightforward descriptions. Bernadotte Schmitt devoted a dozen pages to Jutland, "the most intense drama of World War I," in the prestigious RISE OF MODERN EUROPE series on World War I [413, pp. 138–47]. Hipper's tactical performance was masterful and British errors and omissions determined the indecisive outcome.

John Keegan, who had made a spectacular reputation on military topics with THE FACE OF BATTLE (1976), THE MASK OF COMMAND (1987), and SOLDIERS (1985), then jumped into the naval fray with THE PRICE OF ADMIRALTY (1989) [245], perhaps to his regret. There was also an article [244]. The book was a comparative survey using only secondary sources of three famous naval battles—Trafalgar, Jutland, and Midway— and the battle of the Atlantic against U-boats during World War II: "How men fought at sea in the period from the heyday of the Ship-of-the-Line to the coming of the submarine" (p. 1). He treated Jutland in five phases, separating the battle fleet confrontation into the first and second encounters, criticized Beatty for poor leadership and communications, and proclaimed the list of German technological advantages: better optics, design, construction, guns, projectiles, and strategic posture. Reviewers have praised Keegan for brilliant writing and revelations on the human condition in battle but faulted him for superficial research and numerous errors, e.g., that Jellicoe knew Scheer's position and heading—the reviewer for NIProc claimed 26 mistakes in three pages, pp. 269–72.

"In fact, the battle marked the end of a three and a quarter century reign. Britannia no longer ruled the waves," was the conclusion of Robert O'Connell [327, p. 259]. Edwin Falk [515] cited Jellicoe's excessive caution as the beginning of the end of British hegemony. "The Trafalgar Syndrome" was the title of the analysis of J. A. English [513]. It could have been another Trafalgar but was indecisive.

There were yet other accounts of the battle which should be mentioned. John Buchan [48], in a piece "published by authority" (of whom, it does not say) in 1916, quoted Jellicoe at the end. Rudyard Kipling [255] reminisced in a three-part study of the sea war, the third part of which was about destroyer operations at Jutland, especially at night, but it was mostly popular trivia, including a section on ships' dogs. A 200–page, 5200–line epic poem, an overly dramatic, pro–Evan-Thomas effort, was written by Sir Shane Leslie [267], a friend of Beatty's, and published in 1930. Taprell Dorling [511] was best on destroyer operations. David Howarth [519, pp. 112–27] included Jutland as 1 of 16 famous sea battles in history; Alexander McKee [522] as 1 of 26.

There have been some outstanding "ship biographies": Geoffrey Jones [238] on BARHAM, a QUEEN ELIZABETH class battleship, Hough on AGINCOURT [214], Ross Watton [484], V. E. Tarrant [528], and Stephen Roskill [396] on WARSPITE. The latter ship precipitated a near-disaster at a crucial time when its rudder jammed and it began circling. It has now been determined that the rudder failure, not battle damage, caused the mishap.

A. A. Hoehling [205] summarized naval action during World War I. John Costello [81] and Richard Hough [213] have produced pictorial histories of Jutland. Volume II of THE KEYES PAPERS [172] presented the views of Sir Roger Keyes, who was not at Jutland but who had strong feelings about the controversy.

Richard Hough, who claimed the mantle of Arthur Marder, has written a comprehensive naval history of the war [216]. He may have had access to Marder's research but he has ignored most of the recent scholarship. As with Marder, the hero was Fisher, but Hough was more critical of Jellicoe than was Marder.

Paul Kennedy has produced the most important history of the British navy [251] and his conclusions were that the German claim of victory was misleading and irrevelant; that the summary of a New York newspaper was correct: "The German Fleet has assaulted its jailor but it is still in jail"; and that the simultaneous sorties of the opposing fleets on 19 August 1916 were probably more significant than Jutland because the British effectively evacuated the North Sea due to the submarine menace (pp. 246–47).

In a 1990 article, Colin Lyle [280] asked "Could Germany have Won World War One in an Afternoon?" Scheer's predecessor should have been "maximising the minimum gain"; Scheer was more aggressive but the Germans staked all on the land battle. The British should have been "minimising the maximum gain," and Jellicoe did precisely that.

Innovative methodologies have been incorporated when studying Jutland and associated topics. Sociological model-building was the technique of three articles by John Lambelet [259]. Hugh Neuberger [319] applied quantitative probability analysis to trends in industrial and commercial developments in Germany and Great Britain. Jutland has been the focus of simulation and wargames, e.g., see Hague [167], Dunnigan [512], and "Grand Fleet" [152]. International Business Machines used "Jutland" [241] as the theme in an advertisement in NIProc in 1983. The upshot was that the new IBM anti-submarine warfare system would never leave a commander in a "smoke screen," uninformed, and unprotected. "What if Jellicoe could have seen through it all?" the ad asked.

JELLICOE VS. BEATTY

The Jutland controversy, somewhat simplistically, has evolved into a schism between adherents and supporters of Jellicoe vs. those of Beatty. In the introduction to volume III [297, pp. vii–xiv], Marder concluded that "there has been altogether too much passion and bias," especially regarding "the two British principals. Montagues and Capulets still abound. I am myself neither."

Jellicoe, of course, published his own memoirs [232, 233]. Bacon eventually published an authorized biography of Jellicoe [12]. Edward Altham, captain, RN, was commissioned by the Jellicoe literary trustees to write a biography [4], published in 1938. The family, Frederic Dreyer, J.E.T. Harper, and Bacon's biography [12] were cited as providing assistance. The standard biography of Jellicoe was by A. Temple Patterson [344], who also edited the two–volume JELLICOE PAPERS [345] for the prestigious Navy Records Society [318]. The biography depicted Jellicoe as a gunnery expert and outstanding administrator, not as a strategist or tactician, and as conservative and cautious. Patterson praised Marder's [297] interpretation of Jellicoe and Jutland. Most of the Jellicoe papers came from the collection in the British Library [231]. An appendix to volume II included the Harper papers explaining the making and quashing of the first major investigation of the battle.

John Winton has recently produced a biography [496] which incorporated all of the new interpretations, although, curiously, it has no table of contents nor titles of its 17 chapters. He singled out Beatty's flag lieutenant, Lt. Commander Ralph Seymour, for failures in communication on four different occasions, two at Jutland. He reviewed the controversy between Beatty and Jellicoe.

Correlli Barnett [17, pp. 113–99] characterized Jellicoe as the "sailor with the flawed cutlass," i.e., that British technological development since the mid-nineteenth century was inept and ineffective and that preparation, especially in the matter of education and training for officers, was insufficient and misdirected.

Beatty never published his memoirs, and, for a long time, many of his personal papers were unavailable to scholars; indeed, they were sold at auction. Fortunately, much has been recovered and has now been made available [24]. Beatty has been the subject of several biographies: his nephew, Charles Beatty [21]; Rawson [377]; an authorized one by Chalmers [69], a member of Beatty's staff; and the definitive one by Stephen Roskill [390], who had access to all of the papers, private and public. Bryan Ranft [373] has edited the first of two volumes of Beatty's papers for the Navy Records Society [318]. It covered Jutland and was enlightening on the deterioration of Beatty-Jellicoe relations after the battle. The second volume is forthcoming. Ranft presented a lecture [372] on Beatty as commander-in-chief of the Grand Fleet to the Society for Nautical Research [430] in November 1989.

The Roskill biography [390] has become the definitive one. The third Earl Beatty and others gave Roskill access to all of the personal and private papers so that Roskill demonstrated the charisma, snobbery, anti-Semitism, sexual infidelity, and alcoholism of Beatty. Among the many things about which Marder and Roskill disagreed were primary causes for the British losses and respective assessments of Jellicoe and Beatty. Roskill presented his position as opposed to Marder at length in CHURCHILL AND THE ADMIRALS [391].

A friend of Beatty, Sir Shane Leslie [268], published his memoirs in 1966. Leslie had previously written an unpublished biography [269], and, in LONG SHADOWS, was candid about Beatty's personal life; Beatty's own recollections of Jutland, e.g., his being pleased to learn that Hipper had been forced to abandon his flagship; something that had happened to Beatty at the Battle of Dogger Bank in 1914 where Hipper had commanded; and even Lord Beresford's critique of Jutland. A pro-Beatty encomium by Francis Hunter [222] was in the guise of a four-person collective biography of the "Nelsons of To-day." Beatty received all the credit for Jutland "while Jellicoe merely came on in the third act" (p. 27).

Chapter 6

SOURCES

PUBLIC RECORD OFFICE

This is the largest official repository of all government records. Formerly at Chancery Lane, the Admiralty records were later moved to Kew, near Kew Gardens on the Thames River. Since so many of the German records were either captured and shipped off to Moscow, London, or Washington or destroyed in World War II, the German records held by the British are as extensive as any held anywhere. G. H. Martin, THE RECORDS OF THE NATION [301], contained 15 essays which describe in detail the PRO, its holdings, and services.

Records held there and available to readers are:

Admiralty MSS [1]:

- Adm 1/8460/149—Gunnery Information, Jutland.
  Assessments of the DREADNOUGHT Committee; signed by J. Jellicoe.
- Adm 1/8461/153—Complaint of Vice Admiral Sir David Beatty.
  A letter to the first lord, Arthur Balfour, of 21 June 1916, concerning the dispatches associated with the battles of

Heligoland Bight, Dogger Bank, and Jutland, complaining of distorted descriptions.

- Adm 1/8463/176—"Cause of Explosion in British Warships When Hit by Heavy Shell."
- Adm 1/8484/116 — "Admiralty, HMS MARLBOROUGH in Action, 31 May 1916, List of Casualties, 7 June 1916." A summary of damage and losses.
- Adm 53 series—Log Books.
  Ships' diaries of operations, including all ships of the Royal Navy in all operations, e.g., HMS INVINCIBLE, 1909–1916.
- Adm 116/940B—"Anglo-German Naval Relations, 1902–1914."
  Useful for understanding the naval arms race and general relations.
- Adm 116/1535—"Loss of HMS INVINCIBLE."
- Adm 116/2067—packet on Jutland.
- Adm 137—"Historical Section," 1914–1918 War Histories.
- Adm 137—"Battle of Jutland."
  Contains reports, telegraphic records, original wireless telegraph messages, and various papers.
- Adm 137/1906 and various numbers up to 2151—"The Battle of Jutland, 31 May–1 June 1916."
- Adm 137/1988—"Grand Fleet Intelligence Office Files." General information with emphasis on strategical intelligence, 1914–1918.
- Adm 137/414–430—"The Grand Fleet Narrative," 17 vols. Includes more than the battle of Jutland.
- Adm 137/2129–2134—"The Battle Cruiser Force War Records," 6 vols.
- Adm 137/3839—German High Seas Fleet. "Damage Inflicted on Ships in the Action of 31 May–1 June 1916," by the Naval Intelligence Division, Admiralty War Staff, 13 January 1917.

Details on specific damage on 21 capital ships by name from reports of intelligence agents up to 22 July 1916; later reports confirmed this information as very accurate.

- Adm 186/238—"Progress in Naval Gunnery, 1914–1918."

CABINET OFFICE HISTORICAL SECTION

This archive is now the repository of all matters associated with the Committee of Imperial Defence and the Official War Histories. Its holdings include:

- CID papers.
- Cab 45/269—Jutland.

NATIONAL MARITIME MUSEUM

Located at Greenwich, the Reading Room is the repository for many private papers of prominent naval leaders and other personnel. Catalogues include CATALOGUE OF THE LIBRARY OF THE NATIONAL MARITIME MUSEUM, 3 volumes, London: HMSO, 1972, 1166 pp. [312], and Michael Sanderson, NATIONAL MARITIME MUSEUM CATALOGUE OF THE LIBRARY, 2 volumes, London: HMSO, 1968–1970, 1380 pp. [409].

Among the personal papers of prominent naval leaders are:

- Chatfield MSS, papers of Admiral Lord Chatfield.
- Cowan MSS, papers of Admiral of the Fleet Sir Walter Cowan.
- Dewar MSS, correspondence and papers of Vice Admiral K.G.B. Dewar.
- Duff MSS, diary of Rear Admiral A. L. Duff, commander within the Grand Fleet.
- Oliver MSS, papers of Admiral Sir Henry Oliver, the naval intelligence director.
- Richmond MSS, papers of Admiral Sir Herbert Richmond.
- Tennant MSS, papers of Commander W. G. Tennant, "Jutland," seven lectures.

The museum also contains Imperial German Navy ship plans, the largest extant collection of surviving plans of German warships.

NAVAL LIBRARY, MINISTRY OF DEFENCE

There is a printed catalogue: AUTHOR AND SUBJECT CATALOGUE OF THE NAVAL LIBRARY, Boston: Hall, 1969, 78,000 cards in 5 volumes [314]. Other documents held are as follows: Director of Naval Construction—Admiralty, "Records of Warship Construction During the War, 1914–1918," and Admiralty typescript translation of the GERMAN OFFICIAL HISTORY of the Skagerrak [160].

OTHER ARCHIVES

Some repositories are found in Germany for sources on the battle of Jutland. They are:

- Bundesarchiv-Militararchiv—Militargeschichtliches Forschungsamt Freiburg im Breisgau.
- German Ministry of Marine MSS—includes papers of Admiral Magnus von Levetzow, chief of Operations Section of Admiral Scheer's staff and the post-battle reports of Scheer and Hipper.
- Hipper Nachlasse—private papers of Admiral von Hipper including N162/1-10, Hipper's personal diary, 1914–1919.

Additional holdings can be found in Great Britain. Among these are the following:

British Library (formerly British Museum Library), formerly located on Great Russell Street but moving to King's Cross, London. BL contains the following pertinent sets of papers:

- Balfour MSS—papers of Arthur James Balfour, first lord, 1915–1916, Add MSS 49683–49962, 280 bound volumes or bundles.

- Evan-Thomas MSS—papers of Rear Admiral Hugh Evan-Thomas, commander of the Fifth Battle Squadron.
- Keyes MSS—papers of Admiral of the Fleet Lord Keyes.

Churchill College, Cambridge University—The Churchill College Archive Center has now become an important research center and is the repository for the papers of a long list of important naval leaders and researchers:

- Papers of Fisher, Churchill, A. H. Pollen, Frederic Dreyer, Roskill, and Drax.
- Beatty's BATTLE CRUISER ORDERS—copy in Drax papers.
- Esher papers—Lord Esher, Reginald, Viscount Esher, one of the founders of CID.
- Hankey papers—Sir Maurice Hankey, secretary to CID, and later to the War Cabinet.
- Roskill papers—papers of Stephen Roskill, naval historian, including a copy of NAVAL STAFF APPRECIATION [316] of Jutland.
- Drax papers—papers of Admiral Sir Reginald Aylmer Ranfurly Plunkett-Ernle-Erle Drax, a member of Beatty's staff.
- De Robeck papers—Admiral Sir John De Robeck.
- Hall papers—Admiral Sir Reginald Hall.
- Dreyer papers—Admiral Sir Frederic Dreyer.
- The late George Godfrey-Faussett, son of Eugenie Godfrey-Faussett, mistress of Sir David Beatty, presented 156 intimate letters between Beatty and Mrs. Godfrey-Faussett.

Royal Archives at Windsor Castle. Papers of King George V—correspondence with Sir David Beatty, a good friend of the king.

Imperial War Museum—some papers associated with the war and with Jutland.

Archives of the Beatty family—Beatty papers, Beatty MSS, and other documents held by the third Earl Beatty.

Plus this study: Naval War College, THE BATTLE OF JUT-LAND: 31 May–1 June 1916. Monograph No. 1 Newport, RI: Naval War College, 1921, 148 pp. [18]. An anthology; contains excerpts from German and British official and personal accounts, e.g., von Hase, A. H. Pollen, Scheer, Jellicoe, intelligence surveys, and analyses of operations.

PROFESSIONAL JOURNALS AND PERIODICALS

The following journals and periodicals are most likely to have articles, published documents, review articles, and book reviews associated with the battle of Jutland:

- MM—MARINER'S MIRROR, journal of the Society for Nautical Research, London.
- NAVAL WAR COLLEGE REVIEW, Newport, RI.
- NIProc—PROCEEDINGS OF THE NAVAL INSTITUTE, Annapolis, MD.
- JRUSI— JOURNAL OF THE ROYAL UNITED SERVICES INSTITUTION, London.
  Robin Higham [200] has edited an index to JRUSI, 1857–1963, and there is a catalogue of the RUSI library [401].
- RUSI AND BRASSEY'S DEFENCE YEARBOOK, London. Has also been known as BRASSEY'S NAVAL ANNUAL, THE NAVAL ANNUAL, etc.
- TLS—TIMES LITERARY SUPPLEMENT, London.
- WARSHIP, A quarterly journal, London.
- WARSHIP INTERNATIONAL, A quarterly journal, Toledo, OH.

STANDARD BIBLIOGRAPHIES

- Keith Bird [35]
- Robin Higham [201]
- Edward Homze [208]

- Gerald Jordan [239]
- James Noffsinger [321]
- Eugene L. Rasor [376]
- Myron J. Smith, Jr. [425, 426]
- MARINER'S MIRROR BIBLIOGRAPHY [300]

Appendix

GLOSSARY OF IMPORTANT PERSONS

The primary naval leaders of Great Britain and Germany are identified in more detail as follows:

Balfour, Arthur James, first Earl of Balfour, 1848–1930. Prime Minister, 1902–1905. First lord, 1915–1916.

Beatty, David, first Earl Beatty, 1871-1936. Admiral of the fleet. Commander of the Battle Cruiser force at Jutland and the center of much of the controversy directed against Jellicoe.

Fisher, John "Jacky," Lord Fisher of Kilverstone. Died 1920. Admiral of the fleet. First sea lord, 1904–1910, 1914–1915.

Hipper, Franz Ritter von, 1863–1932. Admiral. Chief of the scouting forces of the High Seas Fleet, WWI, and seen by many as the most dynamic tactician of Jutland.

Jellicoe, John Rushworth, first Earl, 1859–1935. Admiral of the fleet. Commander of the Grand Fleet and later first sea lord.

Scheer, Reinhard, 1863–1928. Admiral. Commander of the High Seas Fleet at Jutland.

Tirpitz, Alfred von, 1849–1930. Admiral of the fleet or gross admiral. Bureaucratic, administrative, and strategic head of the German equivalent to the British Admiralty.

PART II

ANNOTATED BIBLIOGRAPHY

1 Admiralty or Admiralty MSS.
See PRO (Public Record Office).

2 ADMIRALTY NARRATIVE OF THE BATTLE OF JUTLAND.
London: HMSO, 1924.
Issued by the Admiralty; perceived as pro-Beatty and compared to the NAVAL STAFF APPRECIATION [316]; Jellicoe and others objected to some interpretations.

3 Alexander, Arthur Charles Bridgeman. JUTLAND: A PLEA FOR A NAVAL GENERAL STAFF. London: Hugh Rees, 1919, 1923.
By a major; a common complaint about a serious deficiency in the Royal Navy during WWI.

4 Altham, Edward. JELLICOE. ORDER OF MERIT series. London and Glasgow: Blackie, 1938, 200 pp.
Authorized by Jellicoe's literary trustees; access to Jellicoe papers [231] and documents; followed career of "the genius of Jutland"; Marder called it "a good, short biography."

5 Amet, Jacques Marie Albert. LE JUTLAND: BATAILLE NA-VALE DU MAI 31, 1916. [JUTLAND: NAVAL BATTLE OF 31

MAY 1916]. Paris: La Renaissance du Livre, 1923, 144 pp.

Preface by Admiral L. Lacaze, Minister of Marine; a French assessment.

6   Applin, Arthur. ADMIRAL JELLICOE. London: Arthur Pearson, 1915.

A service biography written after Jellicoe became commander of the Grand Fleet but well before Jutland.

7   Aston, Sir George. "Jutland and Mons." CORNHILL MAGAZINE, June 1920.

A naval and a land battle.

8   Aspinall-Oglander, Cecil F. ROGER KEYES: BEING THE BIOGRAPHY OF ADMIRAL OF THE FLEET LORD KEYES OF ZEEBRUGGE AND DOVER. London: Hogarth, 1951, 494 pp.

The authorized biography of a prominent and outspoken admiral, the Dardanelles campaign figure; not at Jutland but involved afterward; Marder [297] called it an "uncritical biography"; see Halpern [172] edition of Keyes papers.

9   Bacon, Sir Reginald Hugh Spencer. THE DOVER PATROL, 1915–1917. 2 vols. London: Hutchinson; New York: Doran, 1919, 716 pp.

A naval squadron providing reconnaissance in force and security for the channel; nothing specifically on Jutland but informative on what other parts of the British navy were doing.

10   Bacon, Sir Reginald Hugh Spencer. FROM 1900 ONWARD. London, 1940, 398 pp.

Foreword by Sir Archibald Hurd; introduction by Sir E.R.G.R. Evans; by one of Jellicoe's most dedicated supporters; Jellicoe: charming disposition and firmness of character; "corrects" account of Jutland by Churchill [73]; indeed, generally denounced Churchill, Lloyd George, and the press; Jellicoe was "kicked out of the Admiralty."

11   Bacon, Sir Reginald Hugh Spencer. THE JUTLAND SCANDAL. London: Hutchinson, 1924, 1925, 176 pp.

"Dedicated to those Two Neglected Goddesses, Justice and Truth, Now Worshipped in an Obscure Corner of the British

Pantheon"; reviewed the literature, or lack of it, which was the "scandal"; Scheer was uncomplimentary to Jellicoe—Scheer said Jellicoe threw away the opportunity to annihilate the High Seas Fleet; Beatty was responsible for the escape of German ships at the earlier battle of Dogger Bank; Beatty responsible for mix-up with Fifth Battle Squadron; Beatty failed to relate vital information to Jellicoe; Patterson [344] called this "belligerently partisan"; Marder [297] saw it as a blast at Jellicoe denigrators but with some substance.

12 Bacon, Sir Reginald Hugh Spencer. LIFE OF JOHN RUSH-WORTH, EARL JELLICOE. London: Cassell, 1936, 581 pp.

Foreword by Reginald McKenna, former first lord; authorized biography; able to ascertain Jellicoe's views before his death; Jellicoe was "through and through a sailor"; four chapters on Jutland, pp. 243–324; concluded deployment problem solved brilliantly; turning away from German torpedo attack saved several battleships; caution was justified for strategic reasons; critical of Beatty.

13 Bacon, Sir Reginald Hugh Spencer. THE LIFE OF LORD FISHER OF KILVERSTONE: ADMIRAL OF THE FLEET. 2 vols. London: Hodder & Stoughton; Garden City: Doubleday, 1929, 640 pp.

First authorized biography; by member of "Fishpond"; lamented that Fisher and Reginald McKenna were not returned together to run the navy during WWI; Balfour made first lord only for political reasons and that hurt effectiveness and efficient management of the navy.

14 Bacon, Sir Reginald Hugh Spencer, Maurice, Sir Frederick, Sydenham, Lord George, Bird, Sir W. D., and Oman, Sir Charles. THE "WORLD CRISIS" BY WINSTON CHURCHILL: A CRITICISM. London: Hutchinson, 1927, 1928, 128 pp.

"Trenchant criticism" of Churchill's lengthy account of Jutland in WORLD CRISIS [73].

15 Bagot, W. T. Translation of the German official account of the battle of Jutland, in volume V of O. Groos, DER KRIEG ZUR SEE, 1914–1918 [THE WAR AT SEA]. Volume V. London, 1926.

See Otto Groos [160], author of German official naval history.

16 "Balfour, Arthur James, first Earl Balfour, 1848–1930." Entry by Algernon Cecil, DNB SUPPLEMENT, 1922–1930. Oxford, Oxford UP, 1937, pp. 41-56.

Balfour much involved in CID and defense matters prior to and during WWI; first lord in coalition government, 1915–1916; "AJB" responsible for controversial post-Jutland communiqué which disseminated a false impression of disaster; characterized Balfour as diffident, unambitious, and insensitive.

17 Barnett, Correlli. THE SWORDBEARERS: SUPREME COMMAND IN THE FIRST WORLD WAR. New York: Morrow, 1963, 1965, 1975, 384 pp.

Collective biography by persistent critic of modern British military-naval leaders; theme: the decisive effect of individual human character on history; four national commanders-in-chief: von Moltke, Philippe Petain, Erich Ludendorff, and Chapter II, "Sailor with the Flawed Cutlass: Admiral Sir John Jellicoe," pp. 101-92; "flawed cutlass" was the Admiralty with no staff, no staff college, no systematic study of naval strategy, and until the Fisher "revolution," "an exclusive yacht club"; leading officers were limp, bewildered, and ineffective; persons with leadership potential had all been sent off to India; Barnett highly critical of Beatty—no wonder that Jellicoe centralized his command; Jutland was a defeat for British technology; at Jutland the German officers were better educated and more capable.

18 BATTLE OF JUTLAND: 31 MAY–1 JUNE 1916. MONOGRAPH NUMBER 1, NAVAL WAR COLLEGE. Newport: Naval War College, 1921, 148 pp.

Collection of pertinent articles and documents assembled for use of the U.S. Naval War College; included short narratives by Jellicoe, Scheer, and Pollen, excerpts from printed accounts by Pollen [359] and Frost [127], and some intelligence analyses.

19 BATTLE OF JUTLAND: 30TH MAY TO 1ST JUNE 1916: OFFICIAL DISPATCHES WITH APPENDICES. Cmd 1068. London: HMSO, 1920, 607 pp.

An early response by the authorities to appease those demanding detailed information about the battle, information repeatedly promised but not forthcoming; included various reports, messages and signals, plans, charts, and diagrams; Marder [297] noted that the messages and signals do not include supplementary information provided by Room 40; some documents of German origin in German, e.g., Admiral Scheer's dispatch.

20 Bayly, Sir Lewis. PULL TOGETHER!: THE MEMOIRS OF ADMIRAL SIR LEWIS BAYLY. London: Harrap, 1939, 300 pp.

Edited by Violet Voysey, a niece; forewords by President Franklin Roosevelt and Admiral Sir Roger Backhouse; Bayly was commander of Allied naval forces; FDR met Bayly during naval inspection in Queenstown in 1918; nothing on Jutland but much on Royal Navy.

21 Beatty, Charles Robert Longfield. OUR ADMIRAL: A BIOGRAPHY OF ADMIRAL OF THE FLEET EARL BEATTY. London: H. H. Allen, 1980, 222 pp.

Personal portrait by son of Beatty's younger brother, David Richard; aimed to project frank and faithful image of an extraordinary character; detailed Beatty's personal life and disastrous marriage; Beatty's papers were sold; noted Chalmers biography [69] not definitive; Stephen Roskill commissioned to publish definitive biography but abruptly dropped because he claimed Beatty had suppressed the HARPER RECORD [182] on Jutland; Roskill [390] later produced the definitive biography.

22 "Beatty, David, first Earl Beatty, 1871-1936." Entry by W. S. Chalmers, DNB SUPPLEMENT, 1931-1940. Oxford: Oxford UP, 1949, pp. 56–64.

Rose rapidly in Royal Navy; youngest flag officer in a hundred years; married Ethel, daughter of Marshall Field; at Jutland, praised for locating enemy and leading it to Grand Fleet; faulted for insufficient and misleading reports to Jellicoe.

23 Beatty's BATTLE CRUISER ORDERS.

Copy in Drax Papers, Churchill College, Cambridge; standard instructions by a squadron commander to the staff and commanding officers on policies and procedures in battle.

24 Beatty Papers. Beatty MSS.

Much of these were sold originally; some have been recovered and are in various locations, e.g., NMM and among third Earl's papers.

25 Beesly, Patrick. ROOM 40: BRITISH NAVAL INTELLI-GENCE, 1914–1918. London: Hamilton; San Diego: Harcourt, Brace, 1982, 349 pp.

Chapter 10 on Jutland, pp. 151–68; access to declassified records; broke German codes; noted director of intelligence, H. F. Oliver, was "workaholic" who refused to delegate; serious delays in getting intelligence to Grand Fleet; in post-Jutland appraisal Room 40 failed to keep Jellicoe informed of vital information; some reform and more success later, for example, in Zimmermann telegram episode.

26 Bellairs, Carlyon. THE BATTLE OF JUTLAND: THE SOWING AND THE REAPING. London: Hodder & Stoughton, 1920, 328 pp.

One of earliest accounts of the battle, by commander, RN; "Dedicated without permission to the man who will give the Royal Navy a Real War Staff"; complained of "suppressed documents"; thus, a need to publish an assessment; critical of Jellicoe, Balfour, and pre-1914 leaders in shrill, accusatory, and outraged manner; chapter critical of "theory of deployment"; Marder [297] noted "patent inaccuracies."

27 Bennett, Geoffrey Martin. THE BATTLE OF JUTLAND. BRITISH BATTLES series. London: Batsford; Philadelphia: Dufour, 1964, 1972, 208 pp.

By captain, RN; excellent historiographical essay: details on HARPER RECORD [182], NAVAL STAFF APPRECIATION [316], and German official history [160] which was critical of Beatty; good on tactical details; noted lack of battle reports to Jellicoe; much intelligence information but not forwarded to Jellicoe; British officers were gallant but not imaginative; defects of British technology due to Fisher's excessive efforts to save money and failure to enlarge drydocks, which caused serious limitations on protection designs; Germans had taken necessary steps in that regard.

28   Bennett, Geoffrey Martin. "The Battle of Jutland." HISTORY TODAY, 10 (May 1960 and June 1960): 313–23 and 395–405.

Two-part presentation; reviewed pro-Jellicoe and pro-Beatty dichotomy; revised NAVAL OPERATIONS [80]; revealed Admiralty blunders; problems created by communiqué; overall, Jutland was indecisive.

29   Bennett, Geoffrey Martin. "The Harper Papers." QUARTERLY REVIEW, 156 (January 1965): 16–25.

Analysis of the Harper MSS at the British Library; the papers of J.E.T. Harper [181].

30   Bennett, Geoffrey Martin. NAVAL BATTLES OF THE FIRST WORLD WAR. BRITISH BATTLES series. London: Batsford; New York: Scribners, 1968, 1969, 320 pp.

Marder [297] called it the first satisfying survey of the naval side of WWI; a tale of lost opportunities; no "der Tag" or repeat of Trafalgar for either side; battleship phase of naval war one of three parts, including overseas and anti-submarine operations.

31   Bennett, Geoffrey Martin. "Scapa Scuttle." NIProc, 85 (August 1959): 533–40.

Disposition of High Seas Fleet which was interned in 1919, thus leaving crews aboard; scuttle was "an act of treachery" which made British navy look ridiculous; real responsibility not that of Royal Navy but Allied Supreme Council for accepting internment instead of surrender; salvage operations continued through 1930.

32   Berghahn, Volcker R. DER TIRPITZ-PLAN: GENESIS UND VERFALL EINER INNENPOLITISCHEN KRISENSTRATEGIE UNTER WILHELM II. [THE TIRPITZ PLAN: GENESIS AND DECLINE OF A DOMESTIC CRISIS STRATEGY UNDER WILHELM II]. Dusseldorf: Droste Verlag, 1971, 640 pp.

Important contribution in Kehr-Fischer "internal-crisis, external-action" controversy; development of doctrine and policy for High Seas Fleet by Tirpitz acting for Wilhelm II; enlightening on naval administration and Tirpitz's machinations.

33   Berghahn, Volcker R. GERMANY AND THE APPROACH OF WAR IN 1914. MAKING OF THE TWENTIETH CENTURY series. New York: St. Martins; London: Macmillan, 1973, 260 pp.

The German volume of an outstanding series, which reviewed all of the latest scholarship and methodologies of the individual big powers just before WWI; chapters on "Tirpitz's Grand Design," "the Anglo-German Naval Arms Race," and the crisis of July 1914; following the Fischer thesis [117] Berghahn called Tirpitz's naval program "an instrument of distraction and social integration . . . to paralyze the pressure for change"; it also provoked the arms race, poisoned the international climate, upset the status quo, created dramatic financial drains on the economy and domestic crises, and provoked the containment of Germany; in his conclusion Berghahn contended that the naval and world policies of Wilhelm II were comprehensive and systematic attempts to upset the international order so as to preserve the domestic balance of power within Germany.

34 Bingham, E.B.S. FALKLANDS, JUTLAND AND THE BIGHT. London: Murray, 1919, 155 pp.

By commander, RN, who served on destroyer HMS NESTOR, which was sunk at Jutland; the crew was picked up by the Germans; introduction by Admiral Sir David Beatty; aboard HMS INVINCIBLE in other two actions; details on destroyer action; no scholarly apparatus.

35 Bird, Keith W. GERMAN NAVAL HISTORY: A GUIDE TO THE LITERATURE. MILITARY HISTORY BIBLIOGRAPHIES series, vol. 7. New York: Garland, 1985, 1152 pp.

Comprehensive bibliography with 800 pages of historiographical narrative and 4871 entries; lamented nothing equivalent to Marder for German navy; extensive references to revisionist Fritz Fischer thesis [117], i.e., in the case of the navy, continuity of ambitions of Tirpitz and Raeder; elaborated on traditionalist-revisionist dichotomy: e.g., Walter Hubatsch [219] vs. Kehr [246], Fischer [117], Berghahn [33], Ivo Lambi [260], and Paul Kennedy [250]; noted Kehr, who was first to analyze naval policy in a scholarly manner, was dismissed as unpatriotic and a "Red."

36 Bowman, Gerald. THE MAN WHO BOUGHT A NAVY: THE STORY OF THE WORLD'S GREATEST SALVAGE ACHIEVEMENT AT SCAPA FLOW. London: Harrap, 1964, 240 pp.

About engineer Ernest F. G. Cox, who purchased and raised the High Seas Fleet scuttled at Scapa Flow; details on scuttling, a thorough and coordinated process; salvage was an eight-year operation, "the greatest feat in the history of marine salvage."

37 Boyle, William Henry Dudley. GALLANT DEEDS: BEING A RECORD OF THE CIRCUMSTANCES UNDER WHICH THE VICTORIA CROSS . . . , 1914–1919. Portsmouth: Gieves, 1919.

By vice admiral, RN; recounted various Victoria Crosses awarded during WWI, including those at Jutland.

38 Bradford, Sir Edward Eden. LIFE OF ADMIRAL OF THE FLEET SIR ARTHUR KNYVET WILSON, BART. London: Murray, 1923.

Biography of one of the most prominent admirals at the time of Jutland; at the Admiralty.

39 Breyer, Siegfried. BATTLESHIPS AND BATTLE CRUISERS, 1905–1970. Garden City: Doubleday, 1973, 480 pp.; orig. SCHLACHTSCHIFFE UND SCHLACHTKREUZER 1905–1970. Muchen: Lehmann, 1970, 507 pp.

Translated from the German by Alfred Kurti; survey of capital ships including an essay on their historical development; 922 schematic illustrations; included conversions; British ships, pp. 125–207, German ships, pp. 276–342; noted deficiencies in design of British battle cruisers; poor translation, some errors, and sweeping claims, especially about German ships.

40 Breyer, Siegfried. BATTLESHIPS OF THE WORLD, 1905–1970. New York: Mayflower, 1980, 557 pp; orig. GROSSKEMPFSCHIFFE 1905–1970. 3 vols. 1977–1979.

Annex to SCHLACHTSCHIFFE UND SCHLACHTKREUZER; 640 illustrations; all ships of all nations.

41 BRITISH VESSELS LOST AT SEA, 1914–1918 AND 1939–1945. London: P. Stephens, 1919, 1947, 1976, 1977, 1988, 395 pp.

Facsimile of four HMSO publications containing details of all ships lost at sea during WWI and WWII.

42 Brown, David K. A CENTURY OF NAVAL CONSTRUCTION: THE HISTORY OF THE ROYAL CORPS OF NAVAL

CONSTRUCTORS, 1883–1983. London: Conway, 1983, 384 pp.

Foreword by duke of Edinburgh; centenary of RCNC by assistant director; mostly about designers and their designs, e.g., Isaac Watts, Baldwin Walker, Cowper Coles, and Sir William White.

43 Brown, David K. "The Design and Construction of the Battleship DREADNOUGHT." WARSHIP, 13 (1980): 39–52.

Fisher got additional ideas from others.

44 Brown, Malcolm and Meehan, Patricia. SCAPA FLOW: THE REMINISCENCES OF MEN AND WOMEN WHO SERVED IN SCAPA FLOW IN THE TWO WORLD WARS. Baltimore: Penguin; London: Lane, 1968, 1969, 264 pp.

Social history–oral history approach; the Grand Fleet was based at this remote base established for the purpose of the "far blockade" of Germany.

45 Brownson, Howard G., "The Technical Aspects of Jutland." NIProc, 60 (1934): 1240–49 pp.

By a lieutenant commander, USN.

46 Bruce, John McIntosh. THE AEROPLANES OF THE ROYAL FLYING CORPS: MILITARY WING. London: Putnams, 1982, 667 pp.

An up-to-date, extensive account of the early airplanes.

47 Bruce, John McIntosh. BRITISH AEROPLANES, 1914–1918. London: Putnams, 1957.

A standard on the aircraft of World War I; detailed specifications.

48 Buchan, John. THE BATTLE OF JUTLAND. London and New York: T. Nelson, 1916, 45 pp.

"Published by authority"; brief account of the battle depicted in four stages and "results": meant no weakening of British naval prestige; quoted Jellicoe at end.

49 Buchan, John. NAVAL EPISODES OF THE GREAT WAR. London: T. Nelson, 1938, 325 pp.

Selections from original four–volume edition, 1921–1922; reviewed important naval operations; Jutland, pp. 221–63; noted Jellicoe's principles and points of dispute.

50 Burt, Ray A. and Trotter, Wilfried Pym. BATTLESHIPS OF THE GRAND FLEET: A PICTORIAL REVIEW OF BRITISH BATTLESHIPS AND BATTLECRUISERS, 1906–1921. Annapolis: NIP, 1982, 96 pp.
  170 illustrations; access to declassified official documents.

51 Burt, Ray A. BRITISH BATTLESHIPS, 1889–1904. Annapolis: NIP, 1988, 320 pp.
  250 illustrations, including detailed schematics; on pre-DREAD-NOUGHTS.

52 Burt, Ray A. BRITISH BATTLESHIPS OF WORLD WAR ONE. London: Arms & Armour; Annapolis: NIP, 1986, 320 pp.
  300 illustrations; began with DREADNOUGHT and the IN-VINCIBLE class battle cruisers, pp. 19–58; also included sections on LION, Beatty's flagship; QUEEN MARY, one of the three lost battle cruisers; and the QUEEN ELIZABETH class battleships of the Fifth Battle Squadron; wealth of detail; access to Admiralty records.

53 Burt, Ray A. BRITISH CRUISERS IN WORLD WAR ONE. WARSHIPS ILLUSTRATED, # 12. Poole: Arms & Armour; New York: Sterling, 1987, 64 pp.
  An illustrated pamphlet containing details on the cruisers which fought at Jutland; part of a series.

54 Burt, Ray A. BRITISH DESTROYERS IN WORLD WAR ONE. WARSHIPS ILLUSTRATED, # 7. Poole: Arms & Armour; New York: Sterling, 1986, 64 pp.
  An illustrated pamphlet containing details on the destroyers which fought at Jutland; part of a series.

55 Burt, Ray A. "The ROYAL SOVEREIGN Class of Battleships, 1913–1948." 3 parts. WARSHIP, 34–36 (1985): 90–96, 176–87, 248–60.
  Successor to QUEEN ELIZABETH Class, eight 15-inch guns, 21 knots, coal/oil propulsion; none at Jutland but several entered service shortly after; prominent during WWII.

56 Butt, F. D. JUTLAND: THE MAIN FEATURES. London: Charterhouse, 1924.
  By commander, RN; preface by Rear-Admiral J.E.T. Harper.

57 Bywater, Hector C. CRUISERS IN BATTLE: NAVAL "LIGHT CAVALRY" UNDER FIRE, 1914–1918. London: Constable, 1939, 292 pp.
Study of cruiser actions during WWI, British and German; interviews and research in archives.

58 Bywater, Hector C. and Ferraby, H. C. STRANGE INTELLIGENCE: MEMOIRS OF NAVAL SECRET SERVICE. London: Constable, 1931, 1934, 308 pp.
By naval journalists; some superficial information about naval intelligence activities; no access to archives.

59 Campbell, N. John M. BATTLECRUISERS: THE DESIGN AND DEVELOPMENT OF BRITISH AND GERMAN BATTLECRUISERS OF THE FIRST WORLD WAR ERA. WARSHIP SPECIAL pamphlet. Greenwich: Conway; New York: Sky, 1978, 72 pp.
By metallurgist and technical expert; for period 1905–1920, defined battle cruiser; protection, i.e., amount and thickness of armor, given lower priority than speed and armament; Germans more successful at producing them; exhaustive treatment of British and German designs; superior-inferior features delineated; by 1930s modernized design and lighter metals meant merger of types of capital ships.

60 Campbell, N. John M. "British Naval Guns, 1880–1945." 18 parts. WARSHIP, 17–38 (1981–1986): various.
By noted expert; massive detail.

61 Campbell, N. John M. JUTLAND: AN ANALYSIS OF THE FIGHTING. London: Conway; Annapolis: NIP, 1986, 447 pp.
Occasion of 70th anniversary of the battle; perhaps the most definitive, detailed, comprehensive, and authoritative survey of the actual events of the battle; by a noted expert metallurgist; assessment of performance on both sides; little on tactics, nothing on strategy; organized by chronological breakdown in five time periods; tracks every shell of every caliber, ammunition expended, damage caused by hits, and damage control; assessed strengths and weaknesses of each fleet; at conclusion, for British, "a thoroughly unsatisfactory battle," for Germans, High Seas

Fleet in no condition to fight for a while; extensive drawings of tracks of ships and gunnery trajectories; curiously, no mention of accounts of Chatfield [72], Pastfield [342], and A. H. Pollen [359].

62 Campbell, N. John M. QUEEN ELIZABETH CLASS BATTLE-SHIPS. WARSHIP MONOGRAPH series. London: Conway, n.d., 50 pp.
Illustrated pamphlet on the latest class of battleships, the ships of the Fifth Battle Squadron; part of a series.

63 Campbell, N. John M. "Washington's Cherrytrees: The Evolution of the British 1921–1922 Capital Ships." 4 parts. WARSHIP, 1–4 (1977): various.
Designs incorporated "lessons" from Jutland; details on disposition of capital ships.

64 Careless, Ronald. BATTLESHIP "NELSON": THE STORY OF HMS "NELSON." London: Arms & Armour, 1985, 160 pp.
One of the post-WWI "Cherrytree" class battleships.

65 Carew, Anthony B. THE LOWER DECK OF THE ROYAL NAVY, 1900–1939: THE INVERGORDON MUTINY IN PERSPECTIVE. Manchester: Manchester UP, 1981, 269 pp.
Best of the social histories of the Royal Navy of the early twentieth century; focused on lower deck reform and organized labor movement among the enlisted men of the navy; began with benefit societies and newspapers; pause in movement during early years of World War I; "Jutland" not in index; militant years, 1919–1923, Invergordon mutiny in 1931; Admiralty oblivious of conditions and rising discontent, then agreed to pay cut in 1931; precipitated mutiny.

66 Carew, Anthony B. "The Royal Naval Lower Deck Reform Movement, 1900–1939." Ph.D. diss., Sussex, 1980.
See book [65].

67 Carver, Sir Michael, ed. THE WAR LORDS: MILITARY COMMANDERS OF THE TWENTIETH CENTURY. London: Weidenfeld & Nicolson; Boston: Little, Brown, 1976, 640 pp.
Only 3 of 43 from Royal Navy; Jellicoe by A. Temple Patterson, pp. 1–12; others include Mountbatten and Cunningham.

68   Chack, de Fregate. "The German Submarines during the Battle of Jutland." NAVAL REVIEW, 13 (November 1925).
By captain, German navy.

69   Chalmers, William S. THE LIFE AND LETTERS OF DAVID, EARL BEATTY, ADMIRAL OF THE FLEET. London: Hodder & Stoughton, 1951, 516 pp.
Introduction by C. S. Forester; by rear-admiral, RN, staff officer of Beatty; authorized biography commissioned by second Earl Beatty; "the greatest fighting admiral in the World War"; Forester reviewed details of marriage scandal; Jutland in chapters 11–13, pp. 220–92.

70   Chalmers, William S. Chalmers MSS.
Included an unfinished MSS. on Jutland by Rear Admiral W. S. Chalmers, 1888–1971.

71   Chatfield, A.E.M., first Baron. BBC Broadcast, March 14, 1941.
Interview and recollections of Admiral Chatfield, 1873–1967.

72   Chatfield, A.E.M., first Baron. THE NAVY AND DEFENCE: THE AUTOBIOGRAPHY OF ADMIRAL OF THE FLEET, LORD CHATFIELD. 2 vols. London: Heinemann, 1942–1947.
Jutland, chapter 15, pp. 138–52; recalled famous assessment after QUEEN MARY blew up: Beatty to Chatfield, Beatty's flag-captain, "There seems to be something wrong with our bloody ships to-day."

73   Churchill, Winston S. THE WORLD CRISIS. 6 vols. (also 4-, 2-, and 1-vol. eds.). New York: Scribners, 1923–1931, 1939, 1951, 1960, 1963 (6 vols., 2800 pp.; 4 vols., 1800 pp.; 2 vols., 1200 pp.; 1 vol., 866 pp.).
Jutland in vol. III; critical of Jellicoe's caution, apparently relying heavily on Dewar's NAVAL STAFF APPRECIATION [316]; added fuel to Jutland controversy; see response by Bacon [14].

74   Claxton, Bernard D., Gurtcheff, John H., and Polles, Jeffrey J. TRAFALGAR AND JUTLAND: A STUDY IN THE PRINCIPLES OF WAR. MILITARY HISTORY MONOGRAPH series. Montgomery: Air Command and Staff College, 1985, 96 pp.

Three faculty members assessed two classic naval battles based on air force principles of warfare.

75 Cocker, Maurice P. DESTROYERS OF THE ROYAL NAVY, 1893–1981. London: Allan, 1981, 136 pp.
200 illustrations; reference guide listing all warships of this category including frigates, sloops, and patrol vessels.

76 Cocker, Maurice P. "OBSERVER'S" DIRECTORY OF ROYAL NAVAL SUBMARINES, 1901-1982. London: F. Warne, 1982, 128 pp.
138 illustrations, drawings by John Lambert; included all submarines in Royal Navy.

77 CONWAY'S ALL THE WORLD'S BATTLESHIPS, 1906 TO THE PRESENT. London: Conway, 1988, 192 pp.
Edited by Ian Sturton; 220 illustrations; authoritative.

78 CONWAY'S ALL THE WORLD'S FIGHTING SHIPS, 1906–1921. London: Conway; Annapolis: NIP, 1984, 1985, 442 pp.
Edited by Robert Gardiner; 950 illustrations; brief mention of Jutland, which was no clear-cut victory.

79 CONWAY'S ALL THE WORLD'S FIGHTING SHIPS, 1922–1946. London: Conway, 1980, 456 pp.
994 illustrations; included ships designed as a result of "lessons" of Jutland.

80 Corbett, Sir Julian S. and Newbolt, Sir Henry. NAVAL OPERATIONS: HISTORY OF THE GREAT WAR: BASED ON OFFICIAL DOCUMENTS. 5 vols. London and New York: Longmans, Green, 1920–1931; second ed., 1938; vol. III, new edition, 1940; 2294 pp. (5 vols.).
By direction of the Historical Section of the Committee of Imperial Defence; vol. III on Jutland completed by Corbett just before his death, then Newbolt took over for vols. IV and V; much controversy over vol. III, published 1923, culminating in "new edition" released in 1940; Admiralty attached formal disclaimer; assessment by James Goldrick [147]: no access to cryptography and secret intelligence, censorship from several quarters, nothing from German perspective; Donald Schurman [415] enlightened on

difficulties faced by Corbett as official historian of controversial naval operations; see Higham [202] on problems of writing official histories.

81　Costello, John and Hughes, Terry. JUTLAND 1916. New York: Holt, Rinehart; London: Weidenfeld & Nicolson, 1976, 1977, 240 pp.
　Mostly pictorial; covered prior Anglo-German naval competition.

82　Cowan, Sir Walter. Cowan MSS.
　Papers of admiral of the fleet at NMM.

83　Coward, Barry R. BATTLESHIPS AND BATTLECRUISERS OF THE ROYAL NAVY SINCE 1861. London: Allan, 1986, 120 pp.
　By commander, RN, who has written some naval fiction; 100–year history from WARRIOR of 1861 to VANGUARD, which was scrapped in 1960.

84　Cowpe, Alan. "Underwater Weapons and the Royal Navy, 1869–1918." Ph.D. diss., King's College, London, 1980, 343 pp.
　Development of torpedo and other underwater weaponry.

85　Cruttwell, C.R.M.F. A HISTORY OF THE GREAT WAR, 1914–1918. Oxford: Clarendon, 1935, 1936, 1969, 1990, 667 pp.
　Extensive, rather personal, and highly opinionated account presenting operations on land and sea; provocative on Jutland, pp. 304–38; mentioned that German submarines were assigned to participate but failed and that the weather precluded zeppelin operations; the problems of the Fifth Battle Squadron were due "to the usual inefficiency of LION's signalling system"; noted "the clumsy truthfulness of our [the British] communiqué"; the Germans were superior in rangefinding, fire direction, night fighting, and in armor protection and watertight integrity because of greater width than British capital ships; finally, claimed that the failure of a decisive British victory at Jutland led to the March Revolution in Russia [!]; coverage of Jutland provoked reactive review in JRUSI 69 (May 1935) and an article (November 1935) by J. Leighton [266]; the reviewer concluded: "If the significance of Jutland still is not apparent, the fault must be due to the pitifully

inefficient way in which news of the battle was broadcast to the world at the time and the gross misrepresentations of the facts then and after the war."

86 Cruttwell, C.R.M.F. THE ROLE OF BRITISH STRATEGY IN THE GREAT WAR. Cambridge: UP, 1936.
Lees-Knowles lectures, Trinity College, Cambridge, 1936.

87 Custer, Benjamin Scott. "Portrait of a Progressive: Lord Fisher, Admiral of the Fleet." NIProc, 73 (March 1947): 255–71.
By captain, USN; superficial summary.

88 Dawson, Robert McGregor. "The Cabinet Minister and Administration: Winston S. Churchill at the Admiralty, 1911–1915." CANADIAN JOURNAL OF ECONOMICS AND POLITICAL SCIENCE, 6 (August 1940): 325–58.
Well-documented analysis of Churchill at Admiralty the first time, presented as an administrative case-study; covered the formative pre-Jutland period.

89 Deacon, Richard. A HISTORY OF THE BRITISH SECRET SERVICE. London: Muller, 1969, 448 pp.
Pseudonym for George D. K. McCormick; began with Tudor period; Room 40 in chapter 17, pp. 203–17; no access to official documents; some fanciful stories.

90 Denniston MSS. Papers of A. G. Denniston.
Churchill College, Cambridge Archive Center.

91 Dewar, A. C. and Dewar, Kenneth G. B. THE NARRATIVE OF JUTLAND. London: HMSO, 1924.
Same as ADMIRALTY NARRATIVE [2]; by two captains, RN; the notorious account denounced by pro-Jellicoe adherents.

92 Dewar, Kenneth G. B. "The Battle of Jutland." 3 parts. NAVAL REVIEW 47 and 48 (October 1959, January 1960, April 1960): various.
Marder [297] called this "trenchant" and containing merit; example of many fine articles in privately circulated NAVAL REVIEW; uncomplimentary to nearly everybody afloat and a-shore, Jellicoe above all.

93 Dewar, Kenneth G. B. Dewar MSS. at NMM.

Diary and correspondence.

94   Dewar, Kenneth G. B. THE NAVY FROM WITHIN. London: Gollanz, 1939, 396 pp.

A personal history of naval developments from about 1900–1930, e.g., the Dardanelles campaign and Jutland, chapter 19, pp. 265–81; especially enlightening perspective on details of various "official" accounts of Jutland; Dewar explained the "history of the history of the battle"; HARPER RECORD [182] began in January 1919; Beatty became first lord and assessed HARPER RECORD as "nothing more than a bald chronological account of the movements . . . [without any] connected narrative," and decided to delay publication; Beatty asked Dewar brothers to formulate account for naval staff college, completed August 1921 [316]; Dewar claimed Bacon [11] himself was responsible for much of capital ship design and gunnery prior to the war, but blamed Beatty for the losses; Dewar insisted Beatty in no way attempted to influence Corbett's NAVAL OPERATIONS [80]; Marder [297] admitted Dewar was excessively critical but also insightful and made important contribution; Hough [213] assessed this as "prejudiced but highly informative."

95   Doenitz, Karl. MEMOIRS: TEN YEARS AND TWENTY DAYS. Cleveland: World; London: Greenhill; Annapolis: NIP, 1959, 1990, 544 pp.

Introduced by Jurgen Rohwer; by grand admiral, German navy; "the last Fuhrer," Hitler's picked successor.

96   D'Ombrain, Nicholas J. "Churchill at the Admiralty and the Committee of Imperial Defense, 1911–1914." JRUSI, 115 (March 1970): 38–41.

Recounted role of Churchill and pre-WWI machinations over imperial defence and war planning; concluded Churchill had no grasp for naval or military strategies but this period at the Admiralty, 1911–1914, was the most formative of Churchill's experience and it molded his life thereafter; enlightening on disposition of CID, which was neglected before and during WWI, and on particular strengths and weaknesses of Admiralty during WWI, e.g., excellent preparation of the battle fleet, but deficient in offensive role and intellectual standards, and unprepared for anti-submarine warfare.

97 D'Ombrain, Nicholas J. WAR MACHINERY AND HIGH POLICY: DEFENCE ADMINISTRATION IN PEACETIME BRITAIN, 1902–1914. OXFORD HISTORICAL MONOGRAPHS. London: Oxford UP, 1973, 319 pp.

Impressive monograph which used extensive primary sources; interaction of defense policy and administration, including the functions of CID, the Admiralty, and the War Office; informative on developments of naval war planning and strategy; credited creation of CID in 1902 to Balfour; early dominated by Lord Esher who oddly held no official position; Fisher supportive for a while; insightful on interdepartmental Army-Navy machinations; critics take D'Ombrain to task for being strong on war machinery but weak on high policy, seen more like "low intrigue"; despite strong leadership of Sir George Clarke and Sir Maurice Hankey, CID never became much-acclaimed General Staff; for another perspective, see F. A. Johnson [235].

98 Dreyer, Sir Frederic C. THE SEA HERITAGE: A STUDY OF MARITIME WARFARE. London: Museum, 1955, 472 pp.

Experiences of Jellicoe's flag-captain, later admiral, RN, from 1891 to post-WWII; chapters 11–13 on Jutland, pp. 111–97; apologist for Jellicoe; detailed infamous "missed signal" from Beatty to Fifth Battle Squadron causing 20–minute delay for that powerful force, and preventing concentration of Beatty's force at most crucial time; noted that Jellicoe received far too little information from all sources during the battle; Marder [297] and Hough [213] attacked poor organization and wordiness but saw as interesting and valuable, especially for Dreyer's perspectives on Jutland.

99 Duff, A. L. Duff MSS.
Diary of Rear-Admiral A. L. Duff at NMM.

100 Dugdale, Blanche E. C. ARTHUR JAMES BALFOUR, FIRST EARL BALFOUR. 2 vols. London and New York: Hutchinson, 1936, 1937, 898 pp.

Official biography of this extraordinary politician and statesman by his niece, who had access to all personal papers; publisher's "blurb" praised AJB as "the most distinguished, the most

discussed and least understood statesman of modern times";
created CID and later served as first lord in coalition government,
May 1915–December 1916, during Jutland; volume II, chapter 8 on
Jutland, pp. 137–65; concerning Jutland communiqué, Admiralty
had little or no word from Grand Fleet from 31 May–2 June, mean-
while, Germans released jubilant claim of victory—for Balfour,
"what to do?"; Balfour decided on "unvarnished statement of
the facts as far as they were known"; Dugdale admitted that
Balfour held a faulty understanding of the psychology of the
common citizen; the communiqué created consternation and
anger throughout Great Britain; eloquent Churchill called in to
attempt salvage effort.

101   Duncan, A. E., Jr. "The Armored Cruiser." NIProc, 85 (July
1959): 86–101.
   Traced pre-WWI development of this predecessor to the battle
cruiser; some participated, and were destroyed, in peripheral
phases of Jutland, and earlier battles of Coronel and the Falklands.

102   Duncan, A. E., Jr. "A Basic Library for the Naval Buff."
NIProc, 86 (August 1960): 120–124.
   For Jutland, recommended Sir Julian Corbett [80] and H. H.
Frost [127], and, overall, other publications such as JANE'S
FIGHTING SHIPS [230] and Stephen Roskill's "single ship bi-
ography" of WARSPITE [396].

103   Dupuy, Richard E. and Dupuy, Trevor N. THE ENCY-
CLOPEDIA OF MILITARY HISTORY: FROM 3500 BC TO THE
PRESENT. New York: Harper & Row, 1970, 1977, 1990, 1526
pp.
   On Jutland, pp. 964–67; outlines four phases, marked the end
of an epoch in naval warfare, the last great fleet action when
enemies could see each other; tactically a draw, but no change
in the strategic situation; neither Jellicoe or Scheer had "the
Nelsonian touch" but Beatty, Hipper, and Captain Hartog of
DERFFLINGER did.

104   Edmonds, Sir James Edward. HISTORY OF THE GREAT
WAR. OFFICIAL HISTORY, 14 vols. London: HMSO, 1922–1947,
1984.
   Official history.

105   Edmonds, Sir James Edward. A SHORT HISTORY OF
WORLD WAR I. New York: Greenwood, 1951, 1968, 488 pp.

Dedicated to Sir Maurice Hankey; outline of former official
history in 14 vols.; mostly on land warfare; treats Jutland, pp. 163–
67, as third of four German High Seas Fleet sorties during
the war.

106   Eggenberger, David. A DICTIONARY OF BATTLES. New
York: Crowell, 1967, 538 pp.

On Jutland, p. 213; the British blockade forced the Germans to
seek a confrontation.

107   Egremont, Lord Max. BALFOUR: A LIFE OF ARTHUR
JAMES BALFOUR. London: Collins, 1980, 391 pp.

More recent official biography, one of several biographies of
the great statesman, first lord of the Admiralty at the time
of Jutland; claimed complete access to personal papers, new
material, and fresh sources; elaborated on AJB's character: "an
impenetrable chasm, a man seemingly devoid of quick passion,
love, attachments, the ordinary vital preoccupations of human-
ity . . . a nihilist. . . . feel[s] nothing"; time as first lord, pp.
259–302; on handling of Jutland communiqué, a contemporary
journalist observed, "Never was a thing so badly handled"; AJB
did prevail upon more sensitive and eloquent Churchill to issue
second statement; persistent problem of AJB, as prime minister
(1902–1906) and as first lord (1915–1916), was indecisiveness, yet
some put him forward to replace Asquith as prime minister in
December 1916.

108   Enser, A.G.S. A SUBJECT BIBLIOGRAPHY OF THE FIRST
WORLD WAR: BOOKS IN ENGLISH, 1914–1978. London:
Deutsch; Boulder: Westview, 1979, 1980, 485 pp.

340 subjects, 5800 entries, cross-references, no annotations.

109   Evan-Thomas, Sir Hugh. Evan-Thomas MSS. British Museum Add. MSS 52504–52506.

Admiral, commander of the Fifth Battle Squadron at Jutland;
much correspondence on the battle.

110   Evans, F. P. "The True Cause of Our Impotence at Jutland."
BLACKWOOD'S MAGAZINE, 221 (April 1927): 427–38.

"Root cause" of naval failures at Jutland was that staffs of Jellicoe and Beatty miscalculated their positions, as much as 11 miles off; critical of Beatty; characterized Grand Fleet tactics as "blind man's bluff."

111   Ewing, Alfred Washington. THE MAN IN ROOM 40: THE LIFE OF SIR ALFRED EWING. London: Hutchinson, 1939, 1940, 295 pp.
By son of founder of Room 40; no access to documents, little about operations.

112   Falls, Cyril B. THE GREAT WAR, 1914–1918. New York: Putnam, 1959, 447 pp.
Rescued some damaged reputations; revisionist view on quality of leadership, especially generals, Allied and German, who were seen as competent and effective; Jutland in chapter 4, pp. 209–19; rejected any comparisons of Jellicoe and Nelson because conditions and risks were so different, e.g., torpedoes, mines, and submarines; Jellicoe needed more than "spirit of Nelson."

113   Falls, Cyril B. WAR BOOKS: AN ANNOTATED BIBLIOGRAPHY OF BOOKS ABOUT THE GREAT WAR. London: Peter Davies; London: Greenhill, 1930, 1990, 350 pp.
Individual annotations, including several about Jutland: R. Bacon [11] and Harper [184] defended Jellicoe; Harper blamed failure on marksmanship and fire control of battle cruisers; Bellairs [26] and Pollen [359] attacked Jellicoe but both written too soon after battle.

114   Fawcett, Harold William and Hooper, Geoffrey W. W., eds. THE FIGHTING AT JUTLAND: THE PERSONAL EXPERIENCES OF FORTY-FIVE OFFICERS AND MEN OF THE BRITISH FLEET. Glasgow: Macmillan; London: Hutchinson, 1920, 1921, 1929, 255 pp.
Oral history accounts; Marder [297] called it an invaluable record; reaction to Admiralty communiqué after the battle.

115   Ferguson, David M. THE WRECKS OF SCAPA FLOW. [n.p.], 1980, 80 pp.
Preface by Admiral Friedrich Ruge; guide to the wrecks.

116 Ferris, John. "Before 'Room 40': The British Empire and Signals Intelligence, 1898–1914." JOURNAL OF STRATEGIC STUDIES, 12 (December 1989): 431–57.
Revision of view that Room 40 originated modern cryptology; extensive codebreaking and cable interception, for example, during Boer War; new light on development of signals intelligence.

117 Fischer, Fritz. GERMANY'S AIMS IN THE FIRST WORLD WAR. New York: Norton; London: Chatto & Windus, 1961, 1964, 1967, 652 pp.
Introduction by Hajo Holborn and James Joll; the original Fritz Fischer thesis; revisionist interpretation of modern German history; stressed "continuity."

118 Fisher, Lord John. MEMORIES AND RECORDS. 2 vols. London: and New York: George Doran, 1919, 1920.
Clearly demonstrated fascinating, exuberant, and dynamic personality of "Jacky" Fisher, the most important naval figure of the era; no outline, no sources cited, no bibliography, no organization, but quite revealing.

119 Fleming, H.M.L. WARSHIPS OF WORLD WAR ONE. 5 vols. London: Allan, 1961.
An obscure compendium.

120 Freiwald, Ludwig. LAST DAYS OF THE GERMAN FLEET. London: Constable, 1932.
By seaman aboard German battleship NASSAU; description of surrender and scuttling.

121 French, David. BRITISH ECONOMIC AND STRATEGIC PLANNING, 1905–1915. London and Boston: Allen & Unwin, 1982, 179 pp.
First of two significant analyses [123] by this University of London professor on the development of the political and administrative bases for war planning and formulation of strategic and economic policies prior to and during WWI; how an ill-prepared nation went to war; the transformation was characterized by using familiar cliches: from "business as usual" to "a nation in arms" to "total war"; broad-based approach and widely acclaimed study.

122   French, David. "British Naval Policy and Strategy, 1889–1912." Unpublished paper to American Historical Association annual meeting, December 1989, San Francisco, on program "The Anglo-German Naval Arms Competition and the Roots of World War I."

Reviewed historiography, including Marder [297]; background for DREADNOUGHT: Fisher aimed for fleet readiness in atmosphere of Edwardian "quest for national efficiency"; see G. R. Searle [418]; thus, DREADNOUGHT to provide technological edge but financial limitations politically imposed meant sacrificing some design and fire control features; see Sumida [444, 445, 449, 451].

123   French, David. BRITISH STRATEGY AND WAR AIMS, 1914–1916. London and Boston: Allen & Unwin, 1986, 288 pp.

Second volume [121] on politics, administration, strategy, and economy of a nation at total war now beginning to look at possibilities for the post-war world; strategy to stop Germany and ensure future security against France and Russia; roles of Sir Edward Grey, Lloyd George, and Lord Kitchener reassessed; stimulating new interpretations; the mid-course, limited strategy to be superseded by later, fight-to-win-at-whatever-cost strategy; volume on 1916–1918 anticipated.

124   Frewen, Oswald M. SAILOR'S SOLILOQUY. London: Hutchinson, 1961, 260 pp.

Edited by G. P. Griggs; diaries, 1887–1910; education and training of young naval officers in RN.

125   Frewen, Oswald M. Frewen MSS. British Museum Add. MSS 53738.

55 vols. of diaries and letters, covering WWI and post-war periods; many letters from Jellicoe about Jutland.

126   Friedman, Norman. BATTLESHIP DESIGN AND DEVELOPMENT, 1904–1945. New York: Mayflower, 1978, 175 pp.

Drawings by John Roberts; detailed schematics and illustrations; some errors and poor index.

127   Frost, Holloway H. THE BATTLE OF JUTLAND. Annapolis: NIP, 1936, 1938, 1964, 1970, 591 pp.

By commander, USN, who had taught at war and staff colleges and who died in 1935, just before publication; completed by Edwin Falk; thorough in-depth study and analysis; interviews and correspondence from Scheer [410], Hipper, von Hase, and Otto Groos [160]; noted background and controversy concerning attaching Fifth Battle Squadron to Beatty's battle cruisers, problems with tactics of destroyers, and influence of weather, i.e., not possible to use airships; "who won?": both fleets maintained relative strengths but battle had "certain unfortunate moral effects" on Grand Fleet and shattered British overconfidence; German communiqué improved German morale; Scheer made tactical errors but deserved credit for escape during night phase; Evan-Thomas and Hood were most effective tactical leaders; Jellicoe conducted the fleet ably but with poor conception of naval warfare; Beatty made numerous errors and had no tactical skill; destroyer operations were unsatisfactory; adequate bibliography.

128 Frost, Holloway H. "A Description of the Battle of Jutland." NIProc, 45 (1919): p. 1829.

An early effort by this young American naval officer; received letters of critique from Scheer, Hipper, and Hase; see vol. 47, p. 1083.

129 Frost, Holloway H. GRANT FLEET UND HOCHSEEFLOT-TE IM WELTKRIEG [GRAND FLEET AND HIGH SEAS FLEET IN THE WORLD WAR]. Berlin: Vorhut, 1938, 568 pp.

German translation of BATTLE OF JUTLAND [127]; foreword by Grand Admiral Erich Raeder.

130 Frothingham, Thomas G. THE NAVAL HISTORY OF THE WORLD WAR. 2 vols. Cambridge: Harvard UP; New York: Books for Library Press, 1924–1925, 1971, 692 pp.

By captain, USN.

131 Frothingham, Thomas G. "The Test of Fact against Fiction in the Battle of Jutland." NIProc, 54 (1928).

By captain, USN.

132 Frothingham, Thomas G. A TRUE ACCOUNT OF THE BATTLE OF JUTLAND. Cambridge: Bacon & Brown, 1920, 1922, 62 pp.

By captain, USN; essential facts, especially after Admiralty delays in publishing official record; to clear up mass of confusion and erroneous narratives.

133 Galster, Karl P. H. ENGLAND, DEUTSCHE FLOTTE UND WELTKRIEG. [BRITAIN, THE GERMAN FLEET AND THE WORLD WAR]. Kiel: J. Scheible, 1925, 200 pp.
A German survey of the naval war.

134 Gemzell, Carl-Axel. ORGANIZATION, CONFLICT, AND INNOVATION: A STUDY OF GERMAN NAVAL STRATEGIC PLANNING, 1888–1940. LUND STUDIES IN INTERNATIONAL HISTORY, # 4. Stockholm: Esselte, 1973, 448 pp.
Analyzed and reviewed naval strategic planning from the time of Wilhelm II to Hitler in a broad sociological and even historiographical setting; saw problems with "mono-causal" explanations, e.g., on the pre-WWI situation, Walter Hubatsch [219] and Gerhard Ritter emphasized the defensive nature of naval planning, and Eckart Kehr [246] and Volker Berghahn [32, 33] linked domestic, constitutional, and naval strategic planning; Gemzell insisted on more complex relationships, e.g., organization, structure, political processes, and peripheral and low-level strata.

135 George, Sidney C. JUTLAND TO JUNKYARD: THE RAISING OF THE SCUTTLED GERMAN HIGH SEAS FLEET FROM SCAPA FLOW: THE GREATEST SALVAGE OPERATION OF ALL TIME. Cambridge: Stevens, 1973, 176 pp.
On Jutland, pp. 16–26; followed individual salvaged ships to ultimate fates.

136 GERMAN MINISTRY OF MARINE MSS. ON THE BATTLE OF SKAGERRAK. Now at Bundesarchiv-Militararchiv Militargeschichtliches Forschungsamt in Freiburg im Breisgau.
Various reports from commanders such as Scheer and Hipper; Marder [297] noted special importance of papers of Admiral Magnus von Levetzow, chief of the Operations Section on Scheer's staff.

137 GERMAN OFFICIAL HISTORY. DER WELTKRIEG. [THE WORLD WAR]. 14 vols.

Official history of WWI.

138 Gibson, Langhorne and Harper, J.E.T. THE RIDDLE OF JUTLAND: AN AUTHENTIC HISTORY. London: Cassell; New York: Coward McCann, 1934, 432 pp.
Introduction by Sir Archibald Hurd, who claimed Jutland was "a predestined event, foretold" and that the "riddle" has now been solved by this work; claimed many false versions based on conjecture and partisanship; this one to be accurate, clear, and unbiased, that "the last word of honest controversy has been written"; explained names given to battle: "Jutland" by Great Britain and "Skagerrakschlacht" or "Skagerrak" by Germany; Gibson and Harper, a captain at the time of HARPER RECORD [182], now a vice admiral, noted lack of intelligence information to Jellicoe; reviewed Admiralty dilemma over announcement communiqué; noted unequal treatment by government concerning honors; sorted out various accounts: HARPER RECORD [182] suppressed by Beatty, but published in 1927; Lloyd George published OFFICIAL DISPATCHES [329] in 1920; "Beatty school" formulated NAVAL STAFF APPRECIATION [316] but never published—actually withdrawn; ADMIRALTY NARRATIVE [2] published in 1924 with Jellicoe's observations as appendix; Scheer published his memoirs [410]; Jellicoe published his memoirs [232, 233]; German official history published [160]; British official history published by CID—Admiralty declined responsibility [80].

139 Giese, Fritz E. KLEINE GESCHICHTE DER DEUTSCHEN FLOTTE [SHORT HISTORY OF THE GERMAN FLEET]. Berlin: Haude & Spenersche, 1966.
A post-WWII survey of German naval history.

140 Giese, Fritz E. "Der Kreuzeradmiral: Admiral Franz Ritter von Hipper, Der Letzte Flottenchef der Kaiserlichen Marine [The Cruiser Admiral: Admiral Hipper, The Last Fleet Commander of the Kaiser's Navy]." SOLDAT UND TECHNIK (1962): 324–25.
A short biography of Admiral Von Hipper.

141 Gilbert, Martin. FIRST WORLD WAR ATLAS. New York: Macmillan; London: Weidenfeld & Nicolson, 1970, 1971, 159 pp.
Widely acclaimed historian and editor of Churchill biography project; some on RN, mostly about the blockade.

142 Gilbert, Martin, ed. WINSTON S. CHURCHILL. 8 vols. Boston: Houghton Mifflin; London: Heinemann, 1962–1988, 8856 pp; Companion volumes containing supporting documents, projected about 20 vols.

Editor of Vols. I & II, Randolph Churchill; pertinent volume was Vol. III, edited by Martin Gilbert, THE CHALLENGE OF WAR, 1914–1916, 1971, 988 pp.; volume began with Churchill in the government, ended with Churchill in the wilderness; Fisher's resignation in May 1915 precipitated the decline which effectively lasted for 25 years; two-thirds of this volume was on Dardanelles campaign and its aftermath; Jutland mentioned three times; it was Asquith who suggested calling in Churchill to draft a more inspiring communiqué after the battle; a footnote stated that Churchill had no other part; Churchill and Fisher did discuss the battle as outside observers; then in 1927, in vol. III of THE WORLD CRISIS [73], Churchill jumped into the Jutland controversy with a 62–page analysis mostly critical of Jellicoe.

143 Gill, Charles Clifford. NAVAL POWER IN THE WAR, 1914–1917. New York: Doran, 1918, 239 pp.

By lieutenant commander, USN; series of lectures at U.S. Naval Academy and contributions to the NEW YORK TIMES CURRENT HISTORY MAGAZINE; for Jutland, chapter 7, "North Sea Battles," pp. 83–119.

144 Gill, Charles Clifford. NAVAL POWER IN THE WAR, 1914–1918. New York: Doran, 1919, 316 pp.

A general survey of the naval war.

145 Gill, Charles Clifford. WHAT HAPPENED AT JUTLAND: THE TACTICS OF THE BATTLE. New York: Doran, 1921, 200 pp.

Described the battle in five phases; 26 diagrams.

146 Godfrey, John H. "Lectures on Jutland." Naval Library, Ministry of Defence.

Admiral, RN, deputy-director, Naval Historical Library; among MSS collections at Naval Library; series of seven lectures on Jutland presented at the Naval Staff College, 1929–1930;

revision of lectures of B. H. Ramsay [371], plus "papers for reference purposes by lecturer"; Marder [297] assessed Godfrey's position as moderate and unbiased.

147 Goldrick, James. THE KING'S SHIPS WERE AT SEA: THE WAR IN THE NORTH SEA, AUGUST 1914–FEBRUARY 1915. Annapolis: NIP, 1984, 371 pp.

By "sailor-scholar," officer in Royal Australian Navy; comprehensive narrative of British and German naval operations in North Sea for first six months of war, the period of "the true beginning of modern naval warfare" when sea warfare occurred in three dimensions and innovations such as the wireless, submarine, aircraft of various forms, mines, and torpedoes were first used in a consistent way; surface actions were at high speed and at long ranges; the RN suffered from an absence of planning and failed to produce a coordinated scheme; the Germans expected a close blockade and were surprised at far blockade; the German navy suffered from a flawed command structure; extensive bibliography.

148 Gollin, Alfred M. THE IMPACT OF AIR POWER ON THE BRITISH PEOPLE AND THEIR GOVERNMENT, 1909–1914. STUDIES IN MILITARY AND STRATEGIC HISTORY. Stanford: UP; London: Macmillan, 1989, 366 pp.

The best account of the coming of air power and preparation for its consequences; Lord Haldane and Winston Churchill played key roles; wide ranging treatment including technical, political, diplomatic, and social aspects; British incapable of producing satisfactory engines; German superiority in airships.

149 Gollin, Alfred M. "THE OBSERVER" AND J. L. GARVIN, 1908–1914: A STUDY IN A GREAT EDITORSHIP. London: Oxford UP, 1960, 445 pp.

Outstanding study of this very influential journalist, editor of the OBSERVER; revealed that Fisher, an adroit propagandist, fed much confidential and detailed information about the navy to Garvin, and, apparently, to other important journalists.

150 Goodenough, Sir William Edmund. BBC Broadcast, 1938.

Interview and recollections of Admiral Goodenough, 1867–1945.

151   Goodenough, Sir William Edmund. A ROUGH RECORD. London: Hutchinson, 1943, 164 pp.

By admiral, RN; on education and training of naval officers, 1870s to 1900; at Heligoland Bight and Jutland, pp. 90–98; light cruiser squadron; cited NAVAL OPERATIONS [80] as most reliable account of Jutland; others, e.g., ADMIRALTY NARRA-TIVE [2] and THE TRUTH ABOUT JUTLAND [184], were colored by opinions, and Bacon [11] and Harper [184] lay too much stress on accuracy of stated positions; presented own perspective from cruiser squadron; Goodenough's own squadron first sighted the High Seas Fleet, and the 16 battleships were reported; gunnery fire opened at 12,000 yards; recalled WARSPITE'S circular antics and the night action.

152   GRAND FLEET: TACTICAL NAVAL COMBAT IN THE NORTH SEA, 1906–1920. Simulation games from Simulation Canada, Bridgewater, Nova Scotia, Canada.

Simulation game providing scenarios from early raids in the North Sea through the end of the war, including, of course, Jutland; available at U.S. $60.00 each.

153   Grant, Robert M. U-BOAT INTELLIGENCE, 1914–1918. Hamden: Archon, 1969, 192 pp.

Detailed and concentrated monograph; on methods to outwit German submarine campaign, including intelligence procedures and sources; used German records; no index.

154   Grant, Robert M. U-BOATS DESTROYED: THE EFFECT OF ANTI-SUBMARINE WARFARE, 1914–1918. London: Putnams, 1964, 172 pp.

By American theologian-naval buff; thoroughly researched but no access to some records; focused on German undersea warfare against the merchant marine and the crisis of 1917; covered various anti-submarine efforts such as mining, Q-ships, and patrols; only belated resort to convoys resolved the crisis; Marder [297] assessed as succinct examination including details of 178 German U-boat losses based on German records.

155   Granville, Wilfred and Kelly, Robin A. INSHORE HEROES: THE STORY OF H. M. MOTOR LAUNCHES IN TWO WORLD WARS. London: Allen, 1961, 320 pp.

On ubiquitous in-shore craft used in channel, North Sea, and Mediterranean, e.g., Dover patrol.

156 Gray, Edwyn. THE DEVIL'S DEVICE: THE STORY OF ROBERT WHITEHEAD, INVENTOR OF THE TORPEDO. Annapolis: NIP; London: Seeley, 1975, 1991, 320 pp.

"The device of the devil," seen as insidious and sneaking, responsible for sinking over 25 million tons of shipping; invented by English engineer working in Austria.

157 Grenfell, Russell. "Sir Robert Arbuthnot at Jutland." JRUSI, 80 (November 1935): 800–804.

Apologist for Arbuthnot, squadron commander of First Cruiser Squadron, killed when HMS DEFENCE blew up at 6:25 PM, 31 May, with 900 lost; sister-ship WARRIOR also heavily damaged; some questions as to why these ships were in such vulnerable positions; some answers included "reckless impetuosity" by Arbuthnot, who obstructed the British battle cruisers; Grenfell denied these accusations, claiming Arbuthnot was properly doing his duty.

158 Griffith, Maurice. THE HIDDEN MENACE: MINE WARFARE, PAST, PRESENT AND FUTURE. Greenwich: Conway, 1981, 159 pp.

Followed development of another of the innovative, sinister weapons introduced in WWI; much detail, written for laymen.

159 Groener, Eric. GERMAN WARSHIPS, 1815–1945. Vol. I: MAJOR SURFACE VESSELS. Annapolis: NIP; London: Conway, 1990, 288 pp.

Projected three volumes; revised by Dieter Jung and Martin Maas; descriptions of 10,000 ships.

160 Groos, Otto. DER KRIEG ZUR SEE, 1914–1918 [THE WAR AT SEA]. 6 vols. Berlin: Mittler & Gohn, 1920–1937, 2394 pp.

The official history of the German navy during the war, "Band 5" on Jutland, DER KRIEG IN DER NORDSEE, JANUARY–JUNE 1916, 588 pp.; Patterson [344] saw it as a German effort to prove victory; admitted extensive damage during second contact of battle fleet phase; more favorable to Jellicoe, e.g.,

praised brilliance of deployment, and agreed with Jellicoe that
ADMIRALTY NARRATIVE [2] was inaccurate on several essential points.

161 Groos, Otto. SEEKRIEGSLEHREN IM LICHTE DES WELT-
KRIEGES [SEA WAR LESSONS IN LIGHT OF THE WORLD
WAR]. Berlin, 1929.
A post-war assessment by the official historian.

162 Guinn, Paul Spencer. BRITISH STRATEGY AND POLITICS,
1914–1918. New York: Oxford UP, 1965, 375 pp.
The traditional British strategy was based on sea power and a
pre-eminent navy, but complications and policies precipitated a
series of great debates: imperial-naval war vs. continental commitment, politicians vs. generals, Easterners vs. Westerners, and
volunteer-military vs. conscription-military.

163 Gusewelle, Jack K. "The Board of Invention and Research:
A Case Study in the Relations between Academic Science and the
Royal Navy in Great Britain during the First World War." Ph.D.
diss., California at Irvine, 1971, 252 pp.
Dissertation under Marder; most pressing issue was research
to find solutions to submarine threat, but other scientific development was also important; Fisher was the leading figure on the
board, and he caused problems, exaggerating the already strained
relationships between the professional naval officers and the
scientific community; BIR laid the foundation for development
of SONAR but cooperative efforts at BIR failed.

164 Hackmann, Willem Dirk. SEEK AND STRIKE: SONAR,
ANTI-SUBMARINE WARFARE, AND THE
ROYAL NAVY, 1914–1954. London: HMSO, 1984, 522 pp.
Demonstrated how the submarine revolutionized naval warfare and what a threat it was to the traditional battle fleet;
semi-official scholarly study of the development of technology
and associated tactics for anti-submarine warfare; details on the
scientific aspects of acoustics and electronics; included history of
the Board of Invention and Research headed by Fisher from 1915;
anti-Fisherites dubbed it "the Board of Intrigue and Revenge,"
revealing some perceptions and the fact of strained relationships
between the civilian scientists and the naval professionals.

165 Hackmann, Willem Dirk. "Underwater Acoustics and the Royal Navy, 1893–1930." ANNALS OF SCIENCE, 36 (May 1979): 255–78.

Under the impetus of the submarine threat, research in underwater acoustics and development of ASDIC, leading to the development of SONAR; included political, scientific, and organizational factors.

166 Haggie, Paul. "The Royal Navy and War Planning in the Fisher Era." JOURNAL OF CONTEMPORARY HISTORY, 8 (July 1973): 113–31.

"INSTANT Readiness for War!" was the characteristically phrased reform objective of Fisher and in many ways that was accomplished prior to WWI; Fisher and Beresford had once envisioned a von Moltke–like "War Lord" of the Admiralty; in practice there was a serious flaw: no mechanisms for war planning functioned properly, no staff, no effective war college, no naval war plans, no "Nelsonian Band of Brothers," no coordination between the navy, CID, and the War Office; Fisher's genius was not strategic; Corbett and Esher, among others, urged him to fill this gap.

167 Hague, Paul. SEA BATTLES IN MINIATURE: A GUIDE TO NAVAL WARGAMING. London: Stevens; Annapolis: NIP, 1980, 160 pp.

An elaborate "how-to" book with 84 illustrations on reconstructing sea battles; Jutland was a favorite wargame battle.

168 Hale, Oron J. GERMANY AND THE DIPLOMATIC REVOLUTION: A STUDY IN DIPLOMACY AND THE PRESS, 1904–1906. Philadelphia: U Pennsylvania P; New York: Octagon, 1931, 1971, 233 pp.

Emphasis on influence of newspaper press and public opinion in Anglo-German relations; naval race was decisive.

169 Hale, Oron J. THE GREAT ILLUSION, 1900–1914. RISE OF MODERN EUROPE series. New York: Harper & Row, 1971, 361 pp.

Typically high quality of scholarship and considered analyses of this series; preliminaries to WWI.

170   Hale, Oron J. PUBLICITY AND DIPLOMACY: WITH SPE-
CIAL REFERENCE TO ENGLAND AND GERMANY, 1890–1914.
New York: Appleton-Century, 1940, 1964, 486 pp.
   Broad coverage of the influence of the newspaper press among
the British and the Germans prior to WWI; Anglo-German naval
competition most important.

171   Halperin, Samuel W. "Anglo-German Naval Rivalry before
the World War." Ph.D. diss., Chicago, 1930.
   An early and detailed study of the naval arms race.

172   Halpern, Paul G., ed. THE KEYES PAPERS: SELECTIONS
FROM PRIVATE AND OFFICIAL CORRESPONDENCE OF AD-
MIRAL OF THE FLEET BARON KEYES OF ZEEBRUGGE. 3 vols.
London: Navy Records Society, 1972–1981, 1469 pp.
   Vols. 117, 121, and 122 of the famous Navy Records Society
series [318]; Keyes to RN at age 13, participated in Anti-Slavery
patrol, Boxer rebellion, Dardanelles campaign, Dover patrol, and,
though not at Jutland, became involved in Beatty-Jellicoe controversy in 1920s; on controversy, vol. II; reviewed and assessed
the various accounts: Jellicoe's [233], NAVAL STAFF APPRECI-
ATION [316], NAVAL OPERATIONS [80], Churchill's account
[73], the German version [160], and a version in the obituary
of Hipper in THE TIMES, 26 May 1932; subsequently member
of Parliament; noisy external critic of Admiralty.

173   Halpern, Paul G. THE MEDITERRANEAN NAVAL SITUA-
TION, 1908–1914. HARVARD HISTORICAL STUDIES, # 86. Cambridge: Harvard UP; London: Oxford UP, 1971, 425 pp.
   From a Harvard dissertation under E. R. May; a brilliant comprehensive study of an important but neglected area prior to
WWI; always overshadowed by threats in the North Sea; naval
competition within the Mediterranean affected Anglo-German
and Anglo-French relations and the strength of British fleets, i.e.,
the "double," "two-keels-to-one," or whatever standard.

174   Halpern, Paul G. THE NAVAL WAR IN THE MEDITER-
RANEAN, 1914–1918. Annapolis: NIP, 1987, 650 pp.
   Continuation of MEDITERRANEAN NAVAL SITUATION [1–
73]; fleet balances in the Mediterranean during wartime; escape
of the German GOEBEN and BRESLAU to Turkey; as in the

case of the North Sea, much anticipation for a major capital ship confrontation; in fact, little capital ship action but much submarine activity; naval operations in complex network involving 12 nations.

175 Halpern, Paul G., ed. THE ROYAL NAVY IN THE MEDITERRANEAN, 1915–1918. Brookfield, VT: Temple Smith, 1987, 638 pp.
Vol. 126 of Navy Records Society publications; relatively unknown operations of RN.

176 Hamilton, W. Mark. THE NATION AND THE NAVY: METHODS AND ORGANIZATION OF BRITISH NAVALIST PROPAGANDA, 1889–1914. New York: Garland, 1986, 419 pp.
From a London School of Economics dissertation; on the "new navalism" prevalent in the 1890s and afterwards; important aspects were rising European-wide movements of militarism, patriotism, and nationalism, concerns about "national efficiency" in Great Britain, naval panics and scares, and a series of influential publicists such as Mahan and Spencer Wilkinson; Fisher contributed to and encouraged these activities.

177 Hamilton, W. Mark. "The 'New Navalism' and the British Navy League, 1895–1914." MARINER'S MIRROR, 64 (February 1978): 37–44.
Aspect of imperialism and naval jingoism conspicuous late in the nineteenth century; led to British Navy League; Fisher often contributed to these propaganda efforts.

178 Hampshire, A. Cecil. THE BLOCKADERS. London: Kimber, 1980, 224 pp.
British blockade efforts in WWI and WWII, an important form of economic warfare; involved large commitment of forces operating under the most severe conditions.

179 Hankey, Sir Maurice. THE SUPREME COMMAND, 1814–1918. 2 vols. London: Allen & Unwin; New York: Macmillan, 1961, 932 pp.
Hankey, later Lord Hankey, was influential in war planning, strategic policy making, and interdepartmental relations as secretary of CID from 1908–1938; from his diary and official documents; see Roskill biography [395].

180 Hardach, Gerd. THE FIRST WORLD WAR, 1914–1918. HISTORY OF THE WORLD ECONOMY IN THE TWENTIETH CENTURY. London: Penguin; Berkeley: U California P, 1977, 344 pp.

One of the best and most detailed analyses on economic and financial aspects of WWI, including arms production, blockading, food supplies, and monetary and fiscal matters.

181 Harper, John Ernest Troyte. Harper MSS. British Museum Add. MSS 54477–54480.

Papers of the first official investigator of the battle; now at British Library, previously at RUSI library; included notes and correspondence of Harper as he was preparing original HARPER RECORD [182], including Harper memo, "Facts Dealing with the Official Record of the Battle of Jutland and the Reason It Was Not Published," reproduced as an appendix to Patterson, JELLICOE PAPERS [345].

182 Harper, John Ernest Troyte. REPRODUCTION OF THE RECORD OF THE BATTLE OF JUTLAND: PREPARED BY CAPTAIN J.E.T. HARPER AND OTHERS IN 1919–1920. Command 2870. London: HMSO, 1927.

By then captain, later admiral, RN; the famous HARPER RECORD, or at least a pale reflection of it, prepared by a special committee after the battle and promised to be released to the public immediately thereafter; withdrawn and suppressed when Beatty became first sea lord; then, in 1927, released by the Admiralty, allegedly in modified form, and with diagrams removed; characterized as "a damp squid" of the original, but with no signs of Admiralty manipulation; supplementary papers associated with it are now at British Library [181].

183 Harper, John Ernest Troyte. THE ROYAL NAVY AT WAR. London, 1941.

Recollections.

184 Harper, John Ernest Troyte. THE TRUTH ABOUT JUTLAND. London: John Murray, 1927, 200 pp.

Not the HARPER RECORD [182] nor THE RIDDLE OF JUTLAND [138], which was co-authored by Harper; told the story of the HARPER RECORD [182], ordered to be prepared by Admiral Lord Webster Wemyss and completed in October 1919, described as "simply a plain, straightforward narrative"; later there were deletions, alterations, and additions; there were delays and various promises about release and publication; THE TRUTH contained a description of the battle, generally pro-Jellicoe, e.g., praising him for the deployment, and restrained on Beatty's actions; Marder [297] assessed it as marred by excessive pro-Jellicoe bias.

185 Hartcup, Guy. THE WAR OF INVENTION: SCIENTIFIC DEVELOPMENTS, 1914–1918. Washington and London: Brassey's, 1988, 238 pp.

On U.S. and British research on weapons, innovations, clashes, and competition, e.g., Pollen vs. the Admiralty [358, Pollen; 451, Sumida]; among the developments were gun fire control, the tank, chemical warfare, and medical advances.

186 Hase, Georg von. KIEL AND JUTLAND. London: Skeffington, 1920, 1921, 1927, 1934, 233 pp.

Translated by Arthur Chambers and F. A. Holt; by captain, German navy, who was first gunnery officer, DERFFLINGER, at Jutland; opened by describing Kiel Week, 1914, a major annual international yachting celebration; cynical tone, bitter about WWI peace settlement; description of Jutland; Marder [297] cited it as a standard source.

187 Hase, Georg von. SKAGERRAK: DIE GROSSTE SEESCHLACHT DER WELTGESCHICHTE. [JUTLAND: THE GREAT SEA BATTLE OF WORLD HISTORY]. Leipzig: K. F. Koehler, 1920, 172 pp.

Authoritative account by German naval captain.

188 Hauser, Oswald. DEUTSCHLAND UND DER ENGLISH-RUSSISCHE GEGENSATZ, 1900–1914. [GERMANY AND THE ANGLO-RUSSIAN CONFLICT]. Gottingen: Musterschmidt, 1958, 296 pp.

Two preoccupations of the British government: fear of German sea power and Russian expansion; claimed German policy-makers failed to appreciate these concerns; Hauser's interpretation was simplistic.

189   Haycock, Ronald and Neilson, Keith, eds. MEN, MACHINES AND WAR. Waterloo: Wilfrid Laurier UP; Atlantic Highlands: Humanities, 1987, 1988, 1989, 216 pp.

Papers from the 11th Military History Symposium, Royal Military College, Kingston, Ontario, March 1984; theme: relationships between technology and war; William H. McNeill, keynote speaker; pertinent paper, "The Royal Navy and Technological Change, 1815–1945," by Professor Jon Sumida of the University of Maryland, pp. 75–92, in which he contended that navies were more influenced by technological change than armies; in the Royal Navy, for example, the effect of the wood-to-steel transformation was profound; change was accelerated during the Fisher era.

190   Hayward, Victor. HMS "TIGER" AT BAY: A SAILOR'S MEMOIR, 1914–1918. London: Kimber, 1977, 190 pp.

Entered RN for 31 years as "Boy" at age 15 in 1913, training at Plymouth; to TIGER for over 6 years, notes large number of suicides and accidental deaths; on Jutland, pp. 93–150; remained in Beatty's squadron, observed High Seas Fleet at Scapa Flow.

191   Head, Brian. "The Hawkcraig Experiments: The Beginnings of Submarine Detection." WARSHIP, 49 (January 1989): 7–16.

At experimental station off Scotland near Firth of Forth, early center of experiments at submarine detection, before ASDIC and SONAR; begun by 1910 Submarine Committee; developed hydrophones.

192   Herwig, Holger H. "Admirals vs. Generals: The War Aims of the Imperial German Navy, 1914–1918." CENTRAL EUROPEAN HISTORY, 5 (September 1972): 208–33.

Study of naval war aims has been neglected; Tirpitz had created a powerful battle fleet and then was shunted aside; in the immediate pre-war period, generals wanted war, admirals, peace; the battle fleet was not included in war planning and aims; in 1916 Commander Wolfgang Wegener [485] formulated a strategic plan for unrestricted submarine warfare with the aim to control the Atlantic Ocean; continuity of war aims in WWII.

193   Herwig, Holger H. "Anatomy of an Arms Race: The German Reaction to HMS DREADNOUGHT." Unpublished paper on program "The Anglo-German Naval Arms Competition and the

Roots of World War I," American Historical Association, 27–30 December 1989, San Francisco.

On program reviewing Anglo-German naval arms race; disputes Jon Sumida's revisionist interpretations [449].

194 Herwig, Holger H. and Heyman, Neil M. BIOGRAPHICAL DICTIONARY OF WORLD WAR I. Westport: Greenwood, 1982, 438 pp.

Useful reference aid; succinct biographical entries for those with high political and military offices; Beatty, pp. 80–81; Hipper, pp. 187–88, a "cold-blooded tactician"; Jellicoe, pp. 196–98, who "did not delegate"; and Scheer, pp. 312–13, who "was not one of the great captains."

195 Herwig, Holger H. "Feudalization of the Bourgeoisie: The Role of the Nobility in the German Naval Officer Corps, 1890–1918." THE HISTORIAN, 38 (February 1976): 268–80.

Tradition and elitism of the Prussian army officer corps carried over into the navy of Tirpitz's time; a German naval historian: "We were a Prussian army-corps transplanted on to iron barracks"; "feudal" within a rapidly changing industrial society; this rigid reactionary stance continued into Nazi era; these were the officers of Jutland and the subsequent mutinies.

196 Herwig, Holger H. THE GERMAN NAVAL OFFICER CORPS: A SOCIAL AND POLITICAL HISTORY, 1890–1914. London: Oxford UP, 1973, 298 pp.

In some ways naval officers were more reactionary, e.g., feudalization of the bourgeoisie, elitist, anti-Semitic, emphasis on a code of honor, the duel, and detrimental to social progress, than the army officers; marred by tensions and unequal treatment of non-executive officers; Friedrich Ruge [404] insisted Herwig exaggerated and misunderstood the social structure of imperial Germany.

197 Herwig, Holger H. "LUXURY FLEET": THE IMPERIAL GERMAN NAVY, 1888–1918. London and New York: Allen & Unwin; Atlantic Highlands: Humanities, 1980, 1987, 316 pp.

Wilhelm II had little grasp of sea power; Tirpitz was a diabolical megalomaniac who persevered with policies which failed—his battle fleet had little effect on the war—and that failure paved the way for mutinies, thus, the battle fleet was an irresponsible luxury; see parallel study by Steinberg [437].

198 Higgins, Maria S. "Winston S. Churchill's Legacy to the Royal Navy, 1911–1915." NAVAL WAR COLLEGE REVIEW, 27 (November 1974): 67–77.

Research paper for the U.S. Naval War College; rightly points to reforms initiated by Churchill on conditions on lower deck and on opportunities for promotion from the ranks; wrong on claim that Churchill had supported strong navy before he became first lord and wrong that Churchill created effective general staff for the navy.

199 Higham, Robin. THE BRITISH RIGID AIRSHIP, 1908–1931. London: Foulis; Westport: Greenwood, 1961, 1975, 426 pp.

About the program which was experimented with but which was abandoned when disaster occurred; airships to be used for reconnaissance; fear of German advantage.

200 Higham, Robin and Wing, Karen. THE CONSOLIDATED AUTHOR AND SUBJECT INDEX TO THE "JOURNAL OF THE ROYAL UNITED SERVICE INSTITUTION", 1857–1963. Ann Arbor: U Microfilms, 1964, 1965, 403 pp.

JRUSI [403] was one of several professional journals which carried a number of significant articles on Jutland.

201 Higham, Robin, ed. A GUIDE TO THE SOURCES OF BRITISH MILITARY HISTORY. CONFERENCE ON BRITISH STUDIES. London: Routledge & Paul; Berkeley: U California P, 1971, 651 pp.

The original and the standard bibliography by all of the experts on 1300 items published up to the late 1960s, and see Jordan [239] for the supplement for more recent publications; critical bibliographical essays; for Jutland see the essay by Marder, "The First World War at Sea," pp. 365–95; for the pre-WWI period, see Ruddock Mackay, "The Navy in the Nineteenth Century, 1854–1914," pp. 238–50.

202 Higham, Robin, ed. OFFICIAL HISTORIES: ESSAYS AND BIBLIOGRAPHIES FROM AROUND THE WORLD. Manhattan: Kansas State University Library, 1970, 656 pp.

The definitive and standard account on the subject of official histories with essays about and lists of the histories of all the important countries of the world; the pertinent essays were Stephen Roskill, "Some Reasons for Official History," pp. 10–19 and P. K. Kemp, "War Studies in the Royal Navy," pp. 481–87; Roskill noted that Corbett in NAVAL OPERATIONS [80] was unable to reveal the story of the decrypted German signals available—but not forwarded—to Jellicoe just prior to Jutland. When the pertinent volume was revised in 1940 reference was made to this and other suppressed information; Roskill also noted that Wemyss and Beatty, as first sea lords, put improper pressure on official historians, e.g., J.E.T. Harper, about the accounts of Jutland and other events, which meant that they were no longer objective historians; Churchill was particularly interested in the official histories of both WWI and WWII.

203 Hiley, Nicholas P. "The Strategic Origins of Room 40." INTELLIGENCE AND NATIONAL SECURITY, 2 (April 1987): 245–73.
     Enlightening details about little-known but extensive activities and operations of naval intelligence before Room 40 was actually set up in 1914.

204 Hodges, Peter. THE BIG GUN: BATTLESHIP MAIN AR-MAMENT, 1860–1945. Annapolis: NIP, 1981, 144 pp.
     A reference work with descriptions, pictures, drawings, details of guns of pre-DREADNOUGHTS and DREADNOUGHTS, ballistics, and caliber-race, from 7 inch to 15 inch.

205 Hoehling, Adolph A. and Hoehling, Mary. THE GREAT WAR AT SEA: A HISTORY OF NAVAL ACTION, 1914–1918. New York: Crowell, 1965, 346 pp.
     Readable, popular account; Jutland, pp. 103–51; "the mightiest naval engagement in history"; admitted need for scholarly-type study of naval actions of WWI.

206 Holloway, S. M. FROM TRENCH AND TURRET: ROYAL MARINES' LETTERS AND DIARIES, 1914–1918. [n.p.], 1987, 103 pp.
     Good sampling of experiences of "blue" and "mud" marines, including some at Jutland.

207   Homer, Francis X. J. and Wilcox, Larry D. GERMANY AND EUROPE BEFORE THE ERA OF THE TWO WORLD WARS: ESSAYS IN HONOR OF ORON JAMES HALE. Charlottesville: U Virginia P, 1986, 280 pp.

Series of essays by former students, including historiographical survey of Anglo-German relations, pp. 27–60, by Eugene Rasor.

208   Homze, Edward L. GERMAN MILITARY AVIATION: A GUIDE TO THE LITERATURE. MILITARY HISTORY BIBLIO-GRAPHIES series, # 2. New York: Garland, 1984, 244 pp.

Typical detailed and "chatty" bibliographical essays, including section on WWI, pp. 29–72; included airships and their operations.

209   Horn, Daniel. THE GERMAN NAVAL MUTINIES OF WORLD WAR I. New Brunswick: Rutgers UP, 1969, 346 pp.

The definitive account in English; access to official documents; concluded that the most serious problem was reactionary officers insensitive to conditions on the lower deck; exposed "myth" that the mutiny was a Communist rebellion.

210   Horn, Daniel, ed. THE PRIVATE WAR OF SEAMAN STUMPF. London: Leslie Freeman, 1969.

Individual case study of High Seas Fleet seaman.

211   Horn, Daniel, ed. WAR, MUTINY AND REVOLUTION IN THE GERMAN NAVY: THE WORLD WAR I DIARY OF SEAMAN RICHARD STUMPF. New Brunswick: Rutgers UP, 1967, 442 pp.

Fascinating diary by perceptive and sophisticated sailor of German navy during WWI.

212   Hough, Richard A. ADMIRAL OF THE FLEET: THE LIFE OF JOHN FISHER. British title: FIRST SEA LORD: AN AU-THORIZED BIOGRAPHY OF ADMIRAL LORD FISHER. New York: Macmillan; London: Allen & Unwin, 1969, 1970, 1977, 392 pp.

Personal and professional biography; access to Fisher papers, reliance on Bacon [11] and Marder [297]; frequently exaggerated, e.g., Fisher as Great Reformer, as prophetic on potential of new weapons, as having "great intellectual powers," and DREAD-NOUGHT as "the greatest single cause of increasing German rivalry at sea"; disappointing, no bibliography.

213 Hough, Richard A. BATTLE OF JUTLAND. London: Hamilton, 1964, 64 pp.

Juvenile format, many pictures; claimed "torpedo" was only undisputed winner at Jutland!; a decisive British victory at Jutland could have prevented the Russian Revolution!; other extraneous items such as the army, land guns, and recruiting!; sadly deficient for the historian who claimed Marder's mantle.

214 Hough, Richard A. THE BIG BATTLESHIP: THE STRANGE STORY OF HMS "AGINCOURT." American title: THE GREAT DREADNOUGHT. London: Joseph; New York: Harper & Row, 1966, 1967, 193 pp.

A ship with an unusual history, belonged to Brazil, Turkey, and Great Britain, which took it over just before WWI; called "the Gin Palace"; in service, 1910–1922; on Jutland, pp. 146–87, in First Battle Squadron; no bibliography.

215 Hough, Richard A. DREADNOUGHT: A HISTORY OF THE MODERN BATTLESHIP. New York: Macmillan; London: Allen & Unwin; New York: Bonanza, 1964, 1968, 1975, 1979, 285 pp.

Introduction by C. S. Forester; dedicated to Oscar Parkes [341]; very large picture book, with 180 illustrations; general account of development of modern battleship; slick, hastily written, strained reading.

216 Hough, Richard A. THE GREAT WAR AT SEA, 1914–1918. New York: Oxford UP, 1983, 1984, 1986, 1987, 353 pp.

Dedicated to Arthur Marder; claimed access to Marder's notes but ignored key sources, e.g., Pollen [358], Kennedy [250], Berghahn [32, 33], and Campbell [59, 61]; Jutland, chapters 12–15, pp. 190–297; contained annotated bibliography; noted dearth of intelligence, signalling failures, praise for Goodenough, Jellicoe's decisiveness in deployment, and Hipper's "death ride."

217 Hovgaard, William. MODERN HISTORY OF WARSHIPS: COMPRISING . . . NAVAL MATTERS. London: Conway; Annapolis: NIP, 1920, 1971, 513 pp.

Foreword by Antony Preston; standard reference work by early twentieth-century naval engineering professor at MIT, originally from Denmark; series of lectures on warship design to 1919.

218   Howarth, David Armine. THE DREADNOUGHTS. Alexandria, VA: Time-Life, 1979, 176 pp.

A popularized account of these early super-battleships.

219   Hubatsch, Walter. DIE ARA TIRPITZ: STUDIEN ZUR DEUTSCHEN MARINEPOLITIK, 1890–1918 [THE TIRPITZ ERA: STUDIES IN GERMAN NAVAL POLICY]. Gottingen: Musterschmidt, 1955, 139 pp.

By leading authority on imperial German navy who was in the conservative camp; Marder [297] described as indispensable for understanding German navy.

220   Hubatsch, Walter. DER ADMIRALSTAB UND DIE OBERSTEN MARINEBEHORDEN, 1848–1945 [THE ADMIRALTY STAFF AND HIGHER NAVAL AUTHORITIES]. Frankfurt: Bernhard & Graefe, 1958, 269 pp.

On role of German admiralty staff.

221   Humble, Richard. BEFORE THE "DREADNOUGHT": THE ROYAL NAVY FROM NELSON TO FISHER. London: Macdonald and Janes, 1976, 224 pp.

General, almost superficial survey of nineteenth-century naval developments; conventional explanations.

222   Hunter, Francis T. BEATTY, JELLICOE, SIMS, AND RODMAN. London: Curtis Brown, 1919, 220 pp.

Introduction by Admiral Hugh Rodman; personal glimpses of "Nelsons of Today"; gave Beatty all of the credit for Jutland, "while Jellicoe merely came on for the third act"; Rodman of U.S. Atlantic Fleet who served under command of Beatty; no index, no bibliography, no notes.

223   Hyatt, A.M.J., ed. "DREADNOUGHT" TO POLARIS: MARITIME STRATEGY SINCE MAHAN. Toronto: Copp Clark; Annapolis: NIP, 1973, 133 pp.

Papers from the Conference on Strategic Studies, University of Western Ontario, March 1972; series of diverse papers by impressive group of naval historians such as Marder, Schurman, Barry Hunt, and Theodore Ropp; see Schurman's essay on Corbett and Ropp's on Tirpitz and German navy.

224 Irving, John James. CORONEL AND THE FALKLANDS. London: Philpot, 1927, 247 pp.

By commander, RN; first and useful account of early naval battles in WWI.

225 Irving, John James. THE SMOKE SCREEN OF JUTLAND. London: Kimber; New York: McKay, 1966, 1967, 256 pp.

By commander, RN, a midshipman at the time of the battle; described problems of gunnery, communications, tactics, and communiqué: "an unpalatable result"; compared Jellicoe to Nelson; Beatty's actions contrary to fleet practices, e.g., disposing the Fifth Battle Squadron; Marder [297] saw it as a graphic account using standard sources.

226 James, Sir William. THE EYES OF THE NAVY: A BIOGRAPHICAL STUDY OF ADMIRAL SIR REGINALD HALL. American title: THE CODE BREAKERS. London: Methuen; New York: St. Martins, 1955, 1956, 238 pp.

By admiral, RN, an intelligence officer during the interwar period who had access to Hall papers; Hall, 1870–1943, director of naval intelligence during WWI; the government refused to permit Hall to publish his autobiography; Hall initiated much deception against Germans and was responsible for the Zimmermann telegram affair.

227 James, Sir William. A GREAT SEAMAN: THE LIFE OF ADMIRAL OF THE FLEET SIR HENRY F. OLIVER. London: Witherby, 1956, 189 pp.

By admiral, RN; authorized biography of prominent admiral who served RN, 1878–1927, based on recollections; recall that Oliver was the Admiralty intelligence-operations officer who seriously erred in properly informing Jellicoe.

228 Jameson, Sir William Scarlett. THE FLEET THAT JACK BUILT: NINE MEN WHO MADE A MODERN NAVY. London: Hart-Davis; New York: Harcourt, Brace, 1962, 344 pp.

By rear-admiral, RN; "Jack" was Fisher (1841–1920), who was most prominently featured among these nine mini-biographies of "fleet builders": Harry Keppel (1809–1904), A. K. Wilson (1842–1921), Lord Beresford (1846–1919), Percy Scott (1853–1924), Jellicoe (1859–1935), Beatty (1871–1936), Tyrwhitt (1870–1951), and

Roger Keyes (1872–1945), subdivided into "forerunners," "builders," and "users"; interesting reading, has bibliography.

229 Jameson, Sir William Scarlett. THE MOST FORMIDABLE THING: THE STORY OF THE SUBMARINE FROM ITS EARLIEST DAYS TO THE END OF WORLD WAR I. London: Hart-Davis, 1965, 280 pp.

By veteran submariner; reviewed developments in various countries, e.g., Fisher perceived potential but ignored efforts for anti-submarine warfare, Tirpitz was late in appreciating the potential, the French were early in experimenting and building; Marder [297] saw as thoroughly researched and best on German U-boat campaign of WWI.

230 JANE'S FIGHTING SHIPS. Alternate title: JANE'S ALL THE WORLD'S FIGHTING SHIPS. London: Jane's. Annual publication since 1898.

An annual compilation with extensive and detailed information on all of the warships of all naval powers; a standard reference guide and reliable source used by naval experts, intelligence operatives, historians, and students of naval warfare; some special reprints, e.g. for 1914.

231 Jellicoe, Sir John Rushworth. "Autobiography." British Museum Add. MSS 49038.

Now at British Library; Marder [297] said this included Jellicoe's critiques of the ADMIRALTY NARRATIVE [2] and of Churchill, WORLD CRISIS, vol. III [73].

232 Jellicoe, Sir John Rushworth. THE CRISIS OF THE NAVAL WAR. London and New York: Cassell, 1920, 349 pp.

Jellicoe's "second volume" [see GRAND FLEET, 233], this one on the U-boat campaign; noted introduction of the convoy system, entry of the U.S., and the sequel.

233 Jellicoe, Sir John Rushworth. THE GRAND FLEET, 1914–1916: ITS CREATION, DEVELOPMENT, AND WORK. London: Cassell, 1919, 524 pp.

"To my comrades of the Grand Fleet"; effectively volume 1 of his two-volume memoirs of his service during WWI; Jellicoe focused on the battle fleet; presented his version of Jutland, pp. 300–414, and the dispatch, pp. 463–89; included many charts and diagrams; Jellicoe revised this book incorporating responses to Jutland controversy but publisher did not accept it.

234 "Jellicoe, John Rushworth, 1859–1935." Entry by Geoffrey Callender, DNB SUPPLEMENT, 1931–1940. Oxford: Oxford UP, 1949, 1975, pp. 474–82.

DNB entry by noted naval historian-bibliographer; noted Jellicoe's early expertise in gunnery and confirmed "correctness of Jellicoe's judgment" on such matters as deployment and turning away from torpedo attacks; on post-battle communiqués: the Germans claimed victory, the Admiralty published "this preposterous claim, supplementing it with a frank but inadequate statement which disclosed little beyond serious losses."

235 Johnson, Franklyn Arthur. DEFENCE BY COMMITTEE: THE BRITISH COMMITTEE OF IMPERIAL DEFENCE, 1885–1959. London: Oxford UP, 1960, 426 pp.

Foreword by Lord Ismay; on origins and formative period of CID; some fault Johnson for giving CID too much prominence and significance prior to and during WWI; credit to Balfour, Esher, and especially Hankey, for revival after WWI; impressive, scholarly study with extensive footnotes and bibliography, but difficult reading.

236 Jones, Archer. THE ART OF WAR IN THE WESTERN WORLD. Urbana: U Illinois P; London: Harrap, 1987, 1988, 764 pp.

Naval warfare got short shrift from Jones; chapter 8, "Apogee of Defence" on WWI, Jutland, pp. 446–47; Jellicoe exerted "commendable caution"; a German tactical victory but they did not come out again—a statement which is not true.

237 Jones, Archer and Koegh, Andrew J. "The DREAD-NOUGHT Revolution: Another Look." MILITARY AFFAIRS, 49 (July 1985): 124–31.

Thesis: the decision to build DREADNOUGHT was made for technological and naval rivalry reasons, which was good, but its speed was a strategic mistake; Percy Scott credited with gunnery revolution; in 1904, appearing before design committee, Fisher stressed long-range accurate fire, fire control over single caliber guns, and speed of 21 knots, an increase of 15% over current maximum; DREADNOUGHT dealt staggering blow to current British and French superiority in pre-DREADNOUGHTS, dramatically devalued those pre-DREADNOUGHTS, and altered the combat value of cruisers.

238 Jones, Geoffrey Patrick. BATTLESHIP "BARHAM." London: Kimber, 1979, 272 pp.

Details and statistics of QUEEN ELIZABETH class battleship which fought at Jutland, eventually lost in November 1941 in the Mediterranean, the only battleship sunk at sea by a U-boat; similar to Roskill "biography" of WARSPITE [396].

239 Jordan, Gerald, ed. BRITISH MILITARY HISTORY: A SUPPLEMENT TO ROBIN HIGHAM'S "GUIDE TO THE SOURCES." MILITARY HISTORY BIBLIOGRAPHIES series, vol. 10. New York: Garland, 1988, 600 pp.

Updated Higham [201], sources published since the late 1960s; bibliographical essays by the experts; 6400 entries; pertinent essay for pre-WWI and Jutland, Jon Sumida, "The Royal Navy, 1860–1919," pp. 213–30; singled out D. K. Brown [42, 43] and N.J.M. Campbell [59, 61] as especially good on materiel; on biographies, Mackay on Fisher [287], Winton [496] on Jellicoe, although Patterson [344] remains more scholarly, Roskill on Beatty [390], Schurman on Corbett [415], and Pollen [358] and Sumida [451] on Pollen; new and good on Jutland, Roskill's BEATTY [390].

240 Jordan, Gerald, ed. NAVAL WARFARE IN THE TWENTIETH CENTURY, 1900–1945: ESSAYS IN HONOUR OF ARTHUR MARDER. London: Croom Helm; New York: Crane Russak, 1977, 243 pp.

Foreword by Earl Mountbatten; dedicated to Arthur Marder; 18 essays by most noted international scholars (British, American, Canadian, Japanese); pertinent essays included Peter Kemp, pp. 16–31, on Admiral Tryon, killed when HMS VICTORIA sank in 1893, but who had already influenced Fisher, A. K. Wilson, and Jellicoe, who brought in needed materiel reform; Ruddock Mackay, pp. 32–44, contributed a historiographical survey on the question of Anglo-German naval rivalry: Woodward [502],

Berghahn [33], related articles by Kennedy [249, 252] (his book, RISE OF ANGLO-GERMAN ANTAGONISM [250], was published in 1987), Padfield [336], Marder [297], Steinberg [437], Fischer [117], Mackay's own biography of Fisher [287], Haggie [166], Herwig [197], Parkes [341], and March [293]; Mackay noted Tirpitz's persistence in his counterproductive policies; exquisite comparative history in the essay by Kennedy, pp. 45–59, who presented biographies of Fisher and Tirpitz, both of whom built impressive new fleets but were "on the sidelines" at the time they were put to wartime use, both were symbols of great maritime conflict, and there were many other startling similarities except in the case of ideological outlooks; Jack Sweetman, pp. 70–89, analyzed the battle of Coronel of 1914, a humiliating defeat by the British squadron off South America, and concluded that poor communications was the primary problem; Higham, pp. 90–104, presented a case study on the rigid airship, which the Admiralty considered but abandoned because of several accidents; Gusewelle, pp. 105–117, a Marder Ph.D. student at California Irvine, recounted the story of the frustrations and failures of the Board of Invention and Research, which experimented in such areas as mines, torpedoes, anti-submarine warfare, communications, and airships; John Slessor, pp. 118–27, used Marder's account of Jutland [297] as a case study on Admiralty command policy: the problems there were higher strategic direction and leadership, problems which were recurrent in both world wars; however, in the Marder account Jellicoe came out best, having been indifferently served by his subordinates, including Beatty, who was incompetent, and by the Admiralty which was guilty of "criminal neglect" for withholding vital information; first and foremost Jellicoe knew he was to retain command of the sea, and he did that; the worst deficiency was lack of a war staff at the Admiralty; other problems at Jutland were the destroyer flotillas, neglect of reconnaissance, a related failure to even consider the use of aircraft for offensive purposes, faulty construction, inferior shells, and faults in the fire control and searchlight systems; the Admiralty failed to learn obvious lessons: even after Jutland, and for decades thereafter, naval authorities continued to be driven by the obsession for a major fleet engagement; the same applied on the failure to use convoys against the U-boat campaigns in both world wars; Peter Gretton, pp. 128–40, reinforced the same argument in his piece on the U-boat campaigns; other essays were just as significant and outstanding but were applicable to other topics and other times, e.g., those of Barry Hunt and Donald Schurman; pp. 186–209; W.A.B. Douglas, pp. 210–32; William Braisted, pp. 167–85; and Sadao Asada, pp. 141–66.

241 "Jutland." Federal Systems Division of International Business Machines (IBM) advertisement. NIProc, 109 (October 1983): 28–29.
   Full schematic, detailed, two-page color advertisement depicting "lessons" of Jutland: Jellicoe uninformed, "in the dark" behind "smoke screen," poor communications. "What if Jellicoe could have seen through it all?" IBM creating a new dimension in anti-submarine warfare (ASW).

242 Kahn, David. THE CODEBREAKERS: THE STORY OF SECRET WRITING. New York: Macmillan, 1967, 1164 pp.; abridged, New York: New American, 1973, 476 pp.
   By journalist expert on cryptology; first comprehensive history of secret communications; Marder [297] praised for skillful use of published sources, for example, on Room 40.

243 Kahn, David. "Codebreaking in World Wars I and II: The Major Successes and Failures, Their Causes and Their Effects." HISTORICAL JOURNAL, 23 (September 1980): 617–39.
   Recounted story of Room 40, the most successful and extensive codebreaking operation of WWI.

244 Keegan, John. "The Battle of Jutland." MILITARY HISTORY QUARTERLY, 1988.
   Popularized version of the battle.

245 Keegan, John. THE PRICE OF ADMIRALTY: THE EVOLUTION OF NAVAL WARFARE. British subtitle: WAR AT SEA FROM MAN OF WAR TO SUBMARINE. London: Hutchinson; New York: Viking, 1988, 1989, 304 pp.
   By former lecturer at Sandhurst; selected four naval battles: Trafalgar, Jutland, pp. 97–156, Midway, and the battle of the Atlantic; with glossary, bibliography, and index; on how men fought at sea before the extinction of the surface ship; stressed

costs of naval warfare in human lives and money; critical that too much emphasis has been placed on capital ships; concluded that the age of the submarine has arrived; account of Jutland, credited Mahan with influencing Wilhelm II to "navalism," meantime, Royal Navy had "grown professionally complacent"; described battle in five phases; Keegan, well known as a brilliant military historian, has been frequently denounced for this amateur-like foray into naval history: Robert Love faults him for numerous errors, thin bibliography, many gaps from best secondary literature, absence of primary research and sources, and no use of scholarly articles and dissertations; Peter Paret faults him for imbalance and absence of an overall thesis; another critic specified 26 different mistakes.

246 Kehr, Eckart. BATTLESHIP BUILDING AND PARTY POLITICS IN GERMANY, 1894–1901. German original: SCHLACHTFLOTTENBAU UND PARTEI-POLITIK, 1894–1901: VERSUCH EINES QUERSCHNITTS DURCH DIE INNENPOLITISCHEN, SOZIALEN UND IDEOLOGISCHEN VORAUSSETZUNGENDES DEUTSCHEN IMPERIALISMUS. Chicago; Berlin; New York: Kraus, 1930, 1965, 1975, 472 pp.

Translated by Pauline R. and E. N. Anderson; by the young German scholar, now rehabilitated, who published in the early 1930s a penetrating, provocative, and judgmental study of the political implications of the German fleet development; a major influence on the later Fritz Fischer thesis [117] and other revisionists of modern German history.

247 Kelly, Patrick James. "The Naval Policy of Imperial Germany, 1900–1914." Ph.D. diss., Georgetown, 1970, 551 pp.

A dissertation under Thomas Helde, using German naval archives; focused on Tirpitz and Tirpitz's motives for developing a battle fleet; concluded Tirpitz was a bureaucratic megalomaniac who persisted against much opposition and reality in pursuing his dream of building a German navy with the potential for imperial expansion and securing a position of power within Germany.

248 Kemp, Peter K., ed. THE PAPERS OF ADMIRAL SIR JOHN FISHER. 2 vols. London: Navy Records Society, 1960–1965.

The amazing and redoubtable Fisher's official papers in which he outlined his plans for design changes of capital ships, modernizing the fleet, and reorganizing squadron dispositions all over the world; in vol. II he revealed plans for reforming naval education and training and other topics, including the background of the Fisher-Beresford controversy which split the Royal Navy; Marder [297] and Bacon [11] had access to these papers.

249   Kennedy, Paul M. "The Development of German Naval Operations Plans against England, 1896–1914." ENGLISH HISTORICAL REVIEW, 89 (January 1974): 48–76.

Recounted a complex and irrational situation among the German naval hierarchy; as Anglo-German relations deteriorated and as the Schlieffen plan developed, the navy was ignored, left to develop its own war plans without official knowledge of what the army and others intended to do; Tirpitz's role was decisive and disruptive; the naval staff continually questioned his strategy, but to no avail.

250   Kennedy, Paul M. THE RISE OF ANGLO-GERMAN ANTAGONISM, 1860–1914. Boston and London: Allen & Unwin, 1980, 1982, 1987, 616 pp.

A detailed structuralist analysis of German and British society, politics, culture, and ideology and a particularly significant new interpretation on the origins and causes of WWI; claimed 10 years of research in 60 archives and incorporated the latest revisionist methodologies in historiography, e.g., structuralism, the Kehr-Fischer PRIMAT DER INNENPOLITIK thesis, and emphasis on the "official mind"; unusual themes which were integrated into the structuralist methodology were domestic politics, pressure groups, religious beliefs, dynastic factors, and Social Darwinism; in both countries during this period there was a general collapse of liberalism and strengthening of imperialism, nationalism, and conservatism; his final conclusion was that there was an "absolute incompatibility of British and German naval aims" and that the German passion for WELTPOLITIK [world domination] was unnecessary and impossible to achieve.

251   Kennedy, Paul M. THE RISE AND FALL OF BRITISH NAVAL MASTERY. New York: Scribners; London: Allen Lane, 1976, 1982, 1986, 405 pp.

The best, most comprehensive, and up-to-date history of the Royal Navy, utilizing all of the latest sources and interpretations; emphasized economic and strategic themes; critique of A. T. Mahan and "navalist" orientation; prefers Halford Mackinder thesis on strategic competition and potential.

252 Kennedy, Paul M. "Tirpitz, England, and the Second Navy Law of 1900: A Strategical Critique." BULLETIN OF THE INSTITUTE OF HISTORICAL RESEARCH, 45 (May 1972): 145–47.

Summary of the Julian Corbett prize essay, 1970; the decisive point of expansion of the German battle fleet, effectively doubling it, from 19 to 38 capital ships; Tirpitz and government propaganda agencies exploited several international incidents to gain support and to force the British to cooperate, a gamble which failed; Tirpitz also hoped to outbuild the British in capital ships, perhaps up to 60 ships, but that, too, failed.

253 Kennedy, Paul M., ed. THE WAR PLANS OF THE GREAT POWERS, 1880–1914. Boston and London: Allen & Unwin, 1979, 1985, 296 pp.

Foreword by Fritz Fischer; 11 essays by scholarly experts on the formulation of war plans by the various big powers prior to WWI; included Paul Haggie, "The Royal Navy and War Planning in the Fisher Era," pp. 118–32, and other essays by Samuel Williamson on France, Jonathan Steinberg on Germany, and a fascinating piece by Paul Kennedy on international cable communications and their disposition as the war broke out—the British immediately cut all of those of the Germans.

254 Keyes, Lord Roger. THE NAVAL MEMOIRS OF ADMIRAL OF THE FLEET SIR ROGER KEYES. 2 vols. London: Thornton-Butterworth, 1934–1935, 816 pp.

By admiral of the fleet, RN, not directly involved in the battle of Jutland but jumped into the controversy afterward; on Jutland, vol. II, pp. 2–4, 19–57; see Halpern, KEYES PAPERS [172].

255 Kipling, Rudyard. SEA WARFARE. New York: Doubleday, Page, 1916, 1917, 222 pp.

The patriotic poet focused on destroyer actions during the battle and recounted a variety of incidents from ramming cruisers at night to descriptions of ship dogs aboard destroyers, "to recapitulate what every one knows."

256   Kocka, Jurgen. FACING TOTAL WAR: GERMAN SOCIE-TY, 1914–1918. Leamington Spa: Berg, 1973, 1984, 286 pp.

Translated by Barbara Weinberger; a comprehensive overview of German society under unique circumstances.

257   Kryske, Lawrence M. ". . . Ruler of the Queen's Navee . . ." NIProc, 99 (January 1973): 72–80.

By midshipman, USN, in an amateur effort; on Winston Churchill, whose only experience before 1911 was as a journalist in colonial actions of the army, who became first lord of the Admiralty in 1911 at a crucial time when naval war plans had been repudiated; Churchill commenced a series of changes of leadership and reforms; claimed Churchill's greatest contribution was decision to shift from coal to oil as the primary fuel for the battle fleet; in fact, that contribution was altered in the next class of battleships, and Churchill's mandate to create an effective general staff was never accomplished.

258   Laffin, John. BRASSEY'S BATTLES: 3500 YEARS OF CON-FLICT, CAMPAIGNS, AND WARS FROM A TO Z. Washington and London: Brassey's, 1986, 497 pp.

Included alphabetical listing of 7000 battles, campaigns, and wars; "Jutland (or Skagerrak to the Germans)" was included, p. 215; presented bare outline of when, where, who, the confrontation, losses, and an assessment: the Germans claimed victory but the strategic balance remained in favor of the British.

259   Lambelet, John C. "The Anglo-German DREADNOUGHT Race, 1905–1914." THE PAPERS OF THE PEACE SCIENCE SO-CIETY, 22 (1974): 1-45.

One of three articles in this special-interest journal, the other two published in vol. 24 (1975) and vol. 26 (1976), dealing with a superficial analysis based on model-building; there were numerous errors.

260   Lambi, Ivo Nikolai. THE NAVY AND GERMAN POWER POLITICS, 1862–1914. Boston and London: Allen & Unwin, 1984, 449 pp.

An exhaustive study on the administrative and political factors in the development of the modern German navy, from before unification to the outbreak of WWI; Tirpitz and the formulation of plans for a battle fleet "emancipated" the navy from the shadows; for a moment, at the turn of the century, the Anglo-German naval race seemed to attain priority status, but, soon, the army resumed first place; the ambitious fleet building program was for nought, and, if anything, actually contributed to the deterioration of Anglo-German relations and the decision by the British to ally with Germany's enemies; Tirpitz executed the massive process but was ignorant of the strategic and political implications; Martin Kitchen described it as an astonishing tale of ineptitude, hubris, and wishful thinking (mostly by Tirpitz and Wilhelm II).

261   Lambton, Antony. THE MOUNTBATTENS: THE BATTEN-BERGS AND YOUNG MOUNTBATTEN. London: Constable, 1989, 256 pp.
Prince Louis Battenberg was first sea lord at the beginning of WWI; eased out because of German heritage.

262   Langhorne, Richard. "The Naval Question in Anglo-German Relations, 1912–1914." HISTORICAL JOURNAL, 14 (June 1971): 359–70.
There were several signs during this crucial period that Anglo-German relations were improving: Churchill and Haldane went to Berlin to negotiate, and there were cooperative endeavors in the Balkans and the Middle East; but emotions remained too high and prominent leaders, e.g., Tirpitz in Germany and Lord Grey and E. Crowe in Britain, obstructed efforts at resolution of conflicts.

263   Layman, R. D. BEFORE THE AIRCRAFT CARRIER: THE DEVELOPMENT OF AVIATION VESSELS, 1849–1922. London: Conway; Annapolis: NIP, 1989, 128 pp.
Foreword by Rear Admiral George van Deurs, USN; by a journalist-aviation buff; covered 73 years of naval aviation development in 10 nations; to adapt aerial devices to the service of naval warfare; as early as 1806 Lord Thomas Chochrane flew

kites from a warship; Austria was first to use aerial devices offensively, in the late 1840s hot air balloons were launched from a warship; the Royal Navy experimented extensively with rigid airships prior to WWI.

264 Layman, R. D. TO ASCEND FROM A FLOATING BASE: SHIPBOARD AERONAUTICS AND AVIATION, 1783–1914. London: Associated UP; Cranbury, NJ: Fairleigh Dickinson UP, 1979, 271 pp.

The "prehistory" of naval aviation; as early as 1783 efforts were made to loft, launch, or tow aerial devices such as kites and balloons; the genesis of the true aircraft carrier was the British-sponsored Ely-Samson flights of 1910–1912.

265 Legg, Stuart, ed. JUTLAND: AN EYE-WITNESS ACCOUNT OF A GREAT BATTLE. London: Hart-Davis; New York: John Day, 1966, 1967, 152 pp.

A collection of British and German eyewitness stories of the battle edited so as to review the events; essentially a book of quotations with no effort at scholarship or to resolve controversies.

266 Leighton, John. "The Historical Perspective of Jutland." JRUSI, 69 (February 1924): 73–83.

Focused on Corbett's account in vol. III, NAVAL OPERATIONS [80], deeming it to be the much-anticipated comprehensive presentation of the battle to the public; reviewed story of previous failures to formulate authentic and complete accounts: the official communique misinformed the public, a "serious mis-statement from the Admiralty," the government published dispatches [329], Jellicoe [233] and Scheer [410] published their accounts, an Admiralty committee, the HARPER RECORD [182], made a study but it was withheld and points of dispute were never divulged, and finally, there was Corbett's official history; Corbett let the facts speak for themselves.

267 Leslie, Sir Shane. JUTLAND: A FRAGMENT OF EPIC. London: Ernest Benn, 1930, 219 pp.

Preface by Commander Augustus Agar; account overdramatized in the form of a 200–page, 5200–line poem; an apologist for Admiral Evan-Thomas of the Fifth Battle Squadron.

268 Leslie, Sir Shane. LONG SHADOWS. London: Murray; Wilkes-Barre: Dimensions, 1966, 1967, 290 pp.

Memoirs of a friend of Beatty and his potential biographer; recalled Beatty and his personal and professional activities, including the unstable wife, the affairs, and the wealth; Beatty reminisced about Jutland, glad he had forced Hipper to change flagships—the reverse occurred at Dogger Bank—thus "tit for tat"; noted that Jutland continued to "hound" Beatty.

269 Leslie, Sir Shane. Biography of Earl Beatty, unpublished MSS.

Recollections of a friend of Beatty.

270 Leyland, John, ed. SOUVENIR OF THE GREAT NAVAL BATTLE AND ROLL OF HONOUR. London: United Newspapers, [1916], 32 pp.

Printed shortly after the battle; included a full-page picture of Beatty, an article on Jellicoe, "Britain's Future Nelson," and an article on Beatty, "the Spirit of Sea Power Incarnate"; other official communiques and summaries; confirmed the view that Beatty was the immediate hero after the battle, but, later, as more details were forthcoming, the popular—and scholarly—support shifted to Jellicoe.

271 Liddell Hart, Basil H. THE REAL WAR, 1914–1918: THE SHORT HISTORY OF THE FIRST WORLD WAR. Boston: Little, Brown, 1930, 508 pp.

A highly critical interpretation of the entire war, and especially of the leadership; all was done incorrectly; on Jutland, pp. 271–95, which he characterized as "Blind Man's Bluff."

272 Liddle, Peter H. THE AIRMAN'S WAR, 1914–1918. London: Blandford, 1987, 200 pp.

Oral history accounts of early air warfare.

273 Liddle, Peter H. THE SAILOR'S WAR, 1914–1918. New York: Sterling; Poole: Blandford, 1985, 224 pp.

Foreword by Sir Charles Hallett; one of a trilogy utilizing Liddle's famous archive at Sunderland Polytechnic containing diaries, letters, photographs, and other personal recollections of the participants in WWI; "to show what it was like for the ratings and junior officers"; included section on Jutland.

274 Liddle, Peter H., ed. HOME FIRES AND FOREIGN FIELDS: BRITISH SOCIAL AND MILITARY EXPERIENCES IN THE FIRST WORLD WAR. New York and London: Brassey's, 1985, 247 pp.

14 essays from a conference to commemorate the 70th anniversary of the outbreak of WWI, September 1984, at Sunderland Polytechnic, location of Liddle's famous archive; pertinent articles included Malcolm Smith, pp. 53–68, on air power; Colin White, "The Navy and the Naval War Considered," pp. 115–34, in which he contended that the navy suffered from a "patronizing negativism," "marred by a deep sense of disappointment," and "the enemy had not been annihilated a la Nelson and Mahan"; these feelings of frustration because of no decisive victory were universal in the RN; more had been written about the "great setpiece of the naval war," Jutland, than any other event; Jutland was "so infuriatingly indecisive" from both sides; but White insisted that there was no justification either for the overall disappointment or the frustration over Jutland: there were major successes, e.g., Room 40, five Victoria Crosses won aboard the anti-submarine Q-ships, and the Anglo-Belgian operations in the East African lakes, and even at Jutland the overall damage to the High Seas Fleet exceeded that of the Grand Fleet: on 1 June the British had 28 battleships in operation, the Germans only 10.

275 Livesey, Anthony. GREAT BATTLES OF WORLD WAR I. London: Michael Joseph, 1989, 200 pp.

Introduction by General Sir Jeremy Moore; many illustrations, depictions, and drawings; on Jutland, pp. 78–91; who won?: the German tilt was exaggerated by the communiqué.

276 Lloyd George, David. WAR MEMOIRS. 6 vols. London: Nicholas & Watson, 1933–1937.

The rising political star of Great Britain at the time of Jutland; soon to be prime minister.

277 LONDON GAZETTE. Third Supplement, 1916.

Traditional way for naval commanders and the Admiralty to officially report on activities, operations, battles, promotions, honors; for December 1916, honors and awards associated with Jutland.

278 Lundeberg, Philip K. "Undersea Warfare and Allied Strategy in World War I." 2 parts. SMITHSONIAN JOURNAL OF HISTORY, 1 (1966).
A survey of a related aspect of naval strategy.

279 Lutzow, A.D. DOGGERBANK—SKAGERRAK: MARINE-ARCHIV. Oldenburg: Gerhard Stalling, 1931, 202 pp.
By admiral, German navy; about two naval battles.

280 Lyle, Colin. "Could Germany Have Won World War One 'in an Afternoon' ?" ARMY QUARTERLY AND DEFENCE JOURNAL, 120 (July 1990): 325–29.
Reacted to statement by Winston Churchill; Lyle assessed the potential of the opposing fleets; the Germans were overly cautious; theory of the British was "minimising their maximum gain," which they did.

281 McInnes, Colin J. and Sheffield, G. D., eds. WARFARE IN THE TWENTIETH CENTURY: THEORY AND PRACTICE. Boston: Unwin Hyman, 1988, 256 pp.
Nine essays on themes of warfare, including Geoffrey Till on naval power, pp. 80–112; short summary of Jutland, noting British disappointment and intelligence and signal failures.

282 Macintyre, Donald G.F.W. JUTLAND. New York: Norton; London: White Lion, 1957, 1958, 1960, 1975, 282 pp.
By captain, RN, great destroyer commander of WWII; included chapter on the controversy; Marder [297] assessed it as a lucid popular work based on standard sources.

283 Macintyre, Donald G.F.W. THE THUNDER OF THE GUNS: A CENTURY OF BATTLESHIPS. New York: Norton; London: Muller, 1959, 1960, 352 pp.
By captain, RN; conventional survey of history of battleships, with introductory chapters on the turret, torpedoes, mines, and DREADNOUGHT; included appendix: "Opposing Fleets at Jutland," pp. 335–38.

284 Macintyre, Donald G.F.W. WINGS OF NEPTUNE: THE STORY OF NAVAL AVIATION. New York: Norton; London: Peter Davies, 1963, 268 pp.
By captain, RN; nothing specifically on Jutland, but background on pioneer days before and during WWI.

285   Mackay, Ruddock F. "The Admiralty, the German Navy, and the Redistribution of the British Fleet, 1904–1905." MM, 56 (August 1970): 341-46.

Fisher to Admiralty, October 1904, and almost immediate redistribution of fleets and other changes; Marder [297] said due to German threat, Fisher had collaborated with journalists who played up that problem; but Mackay contended that Fisher's attitude was ambiguous, the fleet redistribution scheme was a variable response to a series of political-international developments, e.g., the Moroccan crisis, elimination of the Russian navy, and economic dictates, in addition to the rise of the German navy.

286   Mackay, Ruddock F. BALFOUR: INTELLECTUAL STATESMAN. New York and London: Oxford UP, 1985, 388 pp.

Curiously, little on Balfour as first lord.

287   Mackay, Ruddock F. FISHER OF KILVERSTONE. New York and Oxford: Oxford UP, 1973, 539 pp.

By an experienced biographer and widely acclaimed as a more realistic depiction of Fisher, i.e., his reform program was timely and quite effective, the navy was indeed transformed, but his exploits and contributions decreased with time and his methods caused schism and disruption; Mackay was more informative on Fisher's early career, he believed Fisher stayed on too long, the megalomania was obvious after 1900, and the debilitating Fisher vs. Beresford controversy was unnecessary; Fisher concentrated on materiel matters and neglected organizational and strategic concerns; other biographies and editions of Fisher's papers were by Bacon, the official biography [13]; Hough, an "authorized" biography [212]; Kemp [248]; and Marder [295].

288   McKenna, Stephen. REGINALD McKENNA, 1863–1943: A MEMOIR. London: Eyre & Spottiswoode, 1948, 336 pp.

Biography of the first lord during much of the Fisher era; from hindsight, clearly, Fisher-McKenna were a more compatible team than Fisher-Churchill.

289   MacLeod, Roy M. and Andrews, E. Kay. "Scientific Advice in the War at Sea, 1915–1917: The Board of Invention and Research." JOURNAL OF CONTEMPORARY HISTORY, 6 (1971): 3–40.

Another account of the institution involving professional officials and volunteer civilian scientists, headed by Fisher, which was credited with achieving little at the time.

290 McMahon, William E. DREADNOUGHT BATTLESHIPS AND BATTLE CRUISERS. Washington: UP of America, 1978, 318 pp.

A conventional, haphazard presentation; adds nothing new.

291 Mahan, Alfred Thayer. "The Battleship of All-Big-Guns." THE WORLD'S WORK (January 1911): 13898–902.

Mahan was not convinced this was an effective warship.

292 Manning, Thomas D. THE BRITISH DESTROYER. London: Putnams, 1961, 1979, 148 pp.

By captain, RN; originally a "torpedo boat destroyer" of the 1890s; played decisive role at Jutland; reviewed and listed 56 classes of destroyers, 275 schematics and illustrations; March [293] was better and more informative.

293 March, Edgar J. BRITISH DESTROYERS: A HISTORY OF DEVELOPMENT, 1892–1953. London: Seeley; Annapolis: NIP, 1966, 539 pp.

Foreword by Earl Mountbatten; Oscar Parkes [341] was collecting material when he died, at which point March took over; section on Jutland, pp. 234–38; detailed destroyer dispositions; a comprehensive survey including access to Admiralty and builder sources; included 275 plans and illustrations, details on trials, battles, and sea-going experiences; Marder [297] called it "the classic," a veritable encyclopedia.

294 Marder, Arthur J. THE ANATOMY OF BRITISH SEA POWER: A HISTORY OF BRITISH NAVAL POWER IN THE PRE-DREADNOUGHT ERA, 1880–1905. New York: Knopf; Octagon, 1940, 1972, 580 pp.

The standard and definitive account by the most widely acclaimed British naval historian; surveyed the period of maturation of the steam-powered, steel navy supported by public opinion and pressure groups; described the development of the concept of the two-power standard of capital ship construction; noted that navy war plans for an amphibious attack in northern Germany were "diametrically opposed" to those of the army.

295   Marder, Arthur J., ed. FEAR GOD AND DREAD NOUGHT: THE CORRESPONDENCE OF ADMIRAL OF THE FLEET LORD FISHER OF KILVERSTONE. 3 vols. London: Cape, 1952–1959, 1547 pp.

Fascinating, delightful, and revealing reading of the dynamic and outrageous phraseology of the exciting personality of Fisher; Fisher's direct and secret involvement with prominent press leaders came out later; see Gollin [149].

296   Marder, Arthur J. "Fisher and the Genesis of the DREAD-NOUGHT." NIProc, 82 (December 1956): 1309–15.

Details on the formulation of the design of this revolutionary warship; most of the features were not original contributions of Fisher.

297   Marder, Arthur J. FROM "DREADNOUGHT" TO SCAPA FLOW: THE ROYAL NAVY IN THE FISHER ERA, 1904–1919. 5 vols. London and New York: Oxford UP, 1961-1970, 1978, 1900 pp.

If not the most important, certainly the most widely acclaimed work on the history of the Royal Navy; the definitive and standard account of the period before and during WWI; Marder concentrated his scholarly efforts, at least during the first several decades, on researching and writing about the "Fisher era," a term he invented; massive amounts of research among Admiralty and government records and archives in Great Britain, Germany, and the U.S.; a continuation of ANATOMY; vol. III, JUTLAND AND AFTER, revised and updated with new evidence and additional interviews, published 1978, increased from 330 to 389 pp.; the revised edition of vol. III, the only volume revised, included correspondence and interviews with such persons as Sir William James [228], Chalmers [69], Kemp [248], Kennedy [251], Schurman [414], Ruge [404], and, especially, Campbell [61], who informed Marder in an unpublished paper of his research on gunnery and torpedo hits; vol. V, VICTORY AND AFTERMATH, contained a comprehensive annotated bibliography, pp. 346–417, including unpublished papers, official works, published works, and newspapers and periodicals; called Fisher the "father of the materiel school" of naval reformers and admitted Fisher was less interested in tactics and strategy; the "redoubtable 'Jacky' Fisher dominated the navy as it has never been dominated by a single individual"; Marder depicted the Royal Navy as a "drowsy, inefficient, moth-eaten organism" prior to the "new broom" of Fisher; the concept of the DREADNOUGHT was not original with Fisher, e.g., an Italian naval constructor, Colonel Cuniberti, and some earlier American battleship designs, deserved credit; ample background and analysis of the rising Anglo-German naval rivalry; "Fisher era" continued into the 1920s because of the Fisherites Jellicoe, Jackson, Wemyss, and Oliver; Fisher repeatedly hailing Jellicoe as "the future Nelson"; vol. II, YEARS OF POWER, described a navy in a mood of frustration and exasperation just before Jutland; James Goldrick [147] noted Marder was definitive for this period, especially the "war behind the war"; see Sumida [444, 447, 449, 451], Pollen [358], Fairbanks [514], Herwig [518], and Rasor [376] for views which question some of the adulation and glorification of Marder.

298 Marder, Arthur J. "The Influence of History on Sea Power: The Royal Navy and the Lessons of 1914–1918." PACIFIC HISTORY REVIEW, 41 (November 1972): 413–43.
A variation of A. T. Mahan's [291] technique of assessing lessons of sea power.

299 MARINER'S MIRROR: THE JOURNAL OF THE SOCIETY FOR NAUTICAL RESEARCH. Quarterly. London: Cambridge UP, since 1910.
The most prestigious, scholarly journal for naval and maritime topics.

300 MARINER'S MIRROR BIBLIOGRAPHY. Annual. Greenwich: Society for Nautical Research, since 1983.
Compiled annually; lists of books and articles on naval history and broad maritime issues.

301 Martin, G. H. and Spufford, Peter, eds. THE RECORDS OF THE NATION: THE PUBLIC RECORD OFFICE, 1838–1988, THE BRITISH RECORD SOCIETY, 1888–1988. Rochester: Boydell & Brewer, 1990, 320 pp.
15 essays on PRO; included essay on Thirty-Year Rule by Nicholas Cox, pp. 75–86, now the basis for access to government documents.

302 Mayer, Sydney L. and Koenig, W. J. THE TWO WORLD WARS: A GUIDE TO MANUSCRIPT COLLECTIONS IN THE UNITED KINGDOM. London and New York: Bowker, 1976, 329 pp.
Alphabetical listing, Aberdeen City Library to York City Library, of archives, museums, record offices, and libraries where sources on the wars are held.

303 Millett, Allan R. and Murray, Williamson, eds. MILITARY EFFECTIVENESS. MERSHON CENTER SERIES ON INTERNATIONAL SECURITY AND FOREIGN POLICY. 3 vols. Boston: Unwin Hyman, 1988, 1989, 1990, 996 pp.
An ambitious, unified, integrated project, quite rare for anthologies, the three volumes covering respectively WWI, the interwar period, and WWII; each containing a series of essays by 24 experts and organized so that four levels of specific processes—political, operational, strategic, and tactical—were assessed and ranked, even given comparable grades; the pertinent volume, WWI, contained essays, Paul Kennedy on Great Britain, pp. 31–79, Holger Herwig on Germany, pp. 80–115, and a final summary essay by Kennedy, pp. 329–50, on military effectiveness in WWI; in his first essay Kennedy concluded that the British surface warfare North Sea strategy was essentially correct and effective, the commanders knowing that they did not have to steam into dangerous waters, that Jutland revealed many deficiencies, especially the lack of a naval staff, a Fisher legacy, and that Jellicoe's "turn-away" tactic was "an inglorious action, but a sensible strategy"; Herwig assessed German naval strategy as rigid though less complex than the Schlieffen plan, Tirpitz envisioned a single decisive naval battle, there was no staff, no plan, and no coordination or cooperation with the army; because the British did not seek the ultimate battle, the German activities in the North Sea throughout the war were "ad hoc tactical maneuvers"; that the German army and navy experienced strategic bankruptcy early in 1914; in his overall assessment, Kennedy awarded bad grades for military effectiveness to generals and admirals during WWI, indeed, there was much military incompetence, operational expertise had not caught up with the new technology.

304 Moll, Kendall Dean. "Decision Analysis of the British Navy Budget, 1865–1914." Ph.D. diss., Stanford, 1968, 158 pp.

An interdisciplinary exercise using management techniques; overall conclusion was that decisions seemed to be based on budget and philosophical factors rather than on technical, strategic, and economic considerations, or on political party differences.

305 Moll, Kenneth L. "Politics, Power, and Panic: Britain's 1909 DREADNOUGHT 'Gap'. " MILITARY AFFAIRS, 29 (Fall 1965): 133–44.

A major naval panic ensued during the summer and fall of 1909 when it was claimed, wrongly, that the Germans were dramatically accelerating their capital ship building program; the British authorized two DREADNOUGHTS in 1908 and eight in 1909!

306 Moore, John Edward. "Admiralty Politics and the Redistribution of the British Fleet, 1904–1912." Ph.D. diss., Columbia, 1968, 330 pp.

Thesis: that too much emphasis has been placed on Anglo-German naval rivalry and that there were other reasons for this Fisher-inspired redistribution; other factors included the advent of the telegraph and the wireless, financial exigencies, and technological changes, e.g., the torpedo, the destroyer, the submarine, and altered circumstances related to personnel needs; claimed Marder [297] has some factual errors but is still the best account of the period.

307 Mordal, Jacques. TWENTY-FIVE CENTURIES OF SEA WARFARE. London: Souvenir, 1965, 1976, 448 pp.

Translated by Len Ortzen, maps by Michael Fontaine; a general survey; Jutland in chapter 22 of 29 chapters, pp. 263–93.

308 Morison, Elting E. MEN, MACHINES, AND MODERN TIMES. Cambridge: MIT Press, 1966, 244 pp.

An American perspective on the Jacky Fisher revolution, especially in the chapter on gunfire at sea.

309 Moses, John A. THE POLITICS OF ILLUSION: THE FISCHER REVOLUTION IN GERMAN HISTORIOGRAPHY. London: George Prior; New York: Barnes & Noble, 1975, 250 pp.

On how the Kehr [246] and Fischer [117] theses have affected the historiography of modern German history.

310   Moss, Michael S. and Russell, Iain. RANGE AND VISION: THE FIRST HUNDRED YEARS OF BARR AND STROUD. London: Mainstream, 1988, 270 pp.
Important arms producer of Great Britain; especially critical maker of rangefinders and optical instruments used by British warships.

311   Mountbatten of Burma, the Earl. "The Battle of Jutland: An Appreciation Given at the Annual Jutland Dinner in HMS 'WARRIOR' of 25 May 1978." MM, 66 (May 1980): 99–111.
Mountbatten joined HMS LION, Beatty's flagship, seven weeks after the battle when she was under repair; noted British flash and armor-piercing shell problems and comparative superiority of German-built battle cruisers; also noted lack of staff and planning.

312   National Maritime Museum. CATALOGUE OF THE LIBRARY OF THE NATIONAL MARITIME MUSEUM. 3 vols. London: HMSO, 1971, 1166 pp.
Extensive holdings of reading room and library of NMM at Greenwich; contained many papers of prominent naval leaders.

313   NAVAL ANNUAL. See BRASSEY'S NAVAL ANNUAL or RUSI AND BRASSEY'S NAVAL ANNUAL.

314   Naval Library. AUTHOR AND SUBJECT CATALOGUES OF THE NAVAL LIBRARY. Ministry of Defence, London. Boston: Hall, 1968, 78,000 cards in 5 vols.
Extensive holdings of official papers.

315   NAVAL REVIEW INDEX. Vols. 1–64 for years 1913–1976. London: Naval Review, 1978.
"In-house" professional journal for British naval officers.

316   NAVAL STAFF APPRECIATION OF JUTLAND. MONOGRAPHS (HISTORICAL) ADMIRALTY, unpublished.
By two naval captains, brothers A. C. and Kenneth G. B. Dewar; infamous study commissioned by the pro-Beatty Admiralty

"to bring out the battle's lessons"; during the controversy over NAVAL OPERATIONS, the Official History [80], the HARPER RECORD [182], and the ADMIRALTY NARRATIVE [2]; about 300 copies printed but all ordered to be withdrawn, and presumably destroyed, in 1928, but at least three copies survived: among the Harper MSS, British Library; Roskill MSS, Churchill College; and the Library, U. California, Irvine.

317 NAVAL WAR COLLEGE REVIEW. Monthly professional journal. U.S. Naval War College, Newport, RI, since 1948.
   Articles, book reviews, emphasis on professional education.

318 Navy Records Society.
   Since 1893, published collections of naval records and papers, about 130 volumes; highest quality research by pertinent editor-scholars.

319 Neuburger, Hugh and Stokes, Houston H. "The Anglo-German Trade Rivalry, 1887–1913: A Counterfactual Outcome and Its Implications." SOCIAL SCIENCE HISTORY, 3 (Winter 1979): 187–201.
   Trade competition contributed to the deterioration of Anglo-German relations; used quantitative probability analysis to determine that the German trade share would have surpassed the British in 1928 if there had been no war; did the British resort to preventive war, they asked?

320 Newbolt, Henry. A NAVAL HISTORY OF THE WAR, 1914–1918. London: Hodder & Stoughton, [n.d.], 362 pp.
   This volume was planned before Newbolt took over NAVAL OPERATIONS [80], the official naval history, when Corbett died; his thesis stressed the changing nature of warfare, from limited to unlimited; final chapter on Jutland, pp. 341-50.

321 Noffsinger, James P. WORLD WAR I AVIATION BOOKS IN ENGLISH: AN ANNOTATED BIBLIOGRAPHY. Metuchen, NJ: Scarecrow, 1987, 315 pp.
   1663 entries, good annotation for most entries.

322 Norman, Aaron. THE GREAT AIR WAR. New York and London: Macmillan, 1968, 567 pp.
   Unsatisfying account; exaggeration of air war aspects.

323 Norris, Geoffrey. THE ROYAL FLYING CORPS: A HISTO-
RY. London: Muller, 1965, 256 pp.
Foreword by Sir John Slessor; brief bibliography.

324 Nowell-Smith, Simon, ed. EDWARDIAN ENGLAND, 1901–
1914. New York: Oxford UP, 1964, 619 pp.
Fifteen essays without introductory assessment; chapter 13,
"The Royal Navy," by Peter Kemp, pp. 487–516; RN dominated
by "the towering figure" of Fisher; coverage of personnel and
lower deck reforms, Fisher-Beresford schism; critical of Fisher for
destroying spirit of unity, "band of brothers," and cooperation
between army and navy.

325 Occleshaw, Michael E. ARMOUR AGAINST FATE: BRIT-
ISH MILITARY INTELLIGENCE IN THE FIRST WORLD WAR.
Columbus: Ohio UP, 1989, 423 pp.
Emphasis on army and strategic intelligence; informative on
personalities.

326 Occleshaw, Michael E. "British Military Intelligence in the
First World War." Ph.D. diss., Keele, 1984.
The basis for #325.

327 O'Connell, Robert L. OF ARMS AND MEN: A HISTORY OF
WAR, WEAPONS, AND AGGRESSION. New York and Oxford:
Oxford UP, 1989, 377 pp.
The consistent theme was development of weapons; on Jutland,
pp. 256–60, and O'Connell concluded: "In fact, the battle marked
the end of a three-and-a-quarter-century reign. Britannia no longer ruled the waves."

328 Offer, Avner. "Morality and Admiralty: 'Jacky' Fisher, Economic Warfare, and the Laws of War." JOURNAL OF CONTEM-
PORARY HISTORY, 23 (January 1988): 99–119.
British war plans called for a blockade of Germany; RN notorious for ignoring international law and neutrality, a policy
which generated much debate; it did reduce German society to
poverty and was even continued for political reasons into 1919;
thus, Great Britain inflicted unnecessary punishment on German
civilians.

329 OFFICIAL DISPATCHES.

See BATTLE OF JUTLAND [19].

330   Oliver, Sir Henry. Oliver MSS. NMM.
Papers of admiral of the fleet; included "Notes about Room 40."

331   Oram, H.P.K. READY FOR SEA. London: Seeley; Annapolis: NIP, 1974, 260 pp.
Memoirs of service on destroyer OBDURATE in RN; on battle of Jutland, pp. 145–83; "the fog of war, chance, and strange coincidence bedeviled the antagonists and the outcome was indecisive"; OBDURATE in the middle of the early action, observing LION hit and INDEFATIGABLE and QUEEN MARY blown up; recalled that navigation errors were serious—everyone was lost when it was over; Admiralty issued "a deplorable communiqué."

332   Owen, Charles. NO MORE HEROES—THE ROYAL NAVY IN THE TWENTIETH CENTURY: ANATOMY OF A LEGEND. London: Allen & Unwin, 1975, 248 pp.
By a 10-year navy veteran; lamented the end of a more class-oriented structure, the end of the "commander elite"; recounted Fisher-Beresford controversy and mentioned Jellicoe, Beatty, and the Invergordon mutiny.

333   Padfield, Peter. AIM STRAIGHT: A BIOGRAPHY OF ADMIRAL SIR PERCY SCOTT. London: Hodder & Stoughton, 1966, 1967, 317 pp.
A prominent "Fishpond" admiral, a persistent reformer, especially of gunnery and central director fire control matters, who "aimed straight and he hit hard"; a phenomenal ego meant he was too abrasive; predicted that the aircraft and submarine would displace the battleships; Scott had retired before Jutland, but all British capital ships used central director fire control; his 16-year-old-son was killed when DEFENCE blew up.

334   Padfield, Peter. THE BATTLESHIP ERA. London: Hart-Davis; New York: McKay, 1972, 3211 pp.
A conventional history, some omissions, e.g., Pollen fire control innovations, and errors.

335   Padfield, Peter. DOENITZ: THE LAST FUHRER. New York: Harper & Row; London: Gollancz, 1984, 537 pp.

Doenitz in German navy in WWI, a British POW at end.

336   Padfield, Peter. THE GREAT NAVAL RACE: THE ANGLO-GERMAN NAVAL RIVALRY, 1900–1914. New York: McKay; London: Hart-Davis, 1974, 382 pp.

Scholarly researched survey; indicted Tirpitz and Wilhelm II, who were influenced by Mahan and Heinrich von Treitschke; noted that the British adapted to changing conditions and altered imperial, foreign, and strategic policies while the Germans, especially Tirpitz, persisted in blundering into a naval war for which there was no planning or understanding; strained reading.

337   Padfield, Peter. GUNS AT SEA. New York: St. Martins; London: Evelyn, 1972, 1973, 320 pp.

A survey from early times to the present; emphasis on technical and tactical aspects; hero is Sir Percy Scott; critical of Fisher's battle cruiser design.

338   Padfield, Peter. RULE BRITANNIA: THE VICTORIAN AND EDWARDIAN NAVY. Boston and London: Routledge & Paul, 1981, 246 pp.

RN a legendary force with supremacy "unchallengeable," "sea-rulers by birthright"; a conventional survey.

339   Padfield, Peter. SALT AND STEEL. London: Century, 1986, 629 pp.

A novel about a Hampstead family during the first two decades of this century, including life in the Royal Navy and effects of WWI.

340   Palmer, Joseph and Norris, John G. "Naval Air: The British Experience." SEA POWER, 16 (February 1973): 8–19.

History of Fleet Air Arm and early experiments; authorities not impressed and continued to stress, and build, battleships.

341   Parkes, Oscar. BRITISH BATTLESHIPS: "WARRIOR" 1860 TO "VANGUARD" 1950: A HISTORY OF DESIGN, CONSTRUCTION AND ARMAMENT. London: Seeley, 1957, 1958, 1972, 1990, 701 pp.

Foreword by Earl Mountbatten; 450 illustrations; presented the evolution of the battleship, including plans, designs, and photographs; comprehensive.

342 Pastfield, John L. NEW LIGHT ON JUTLAND. London: Heinemann, 1933, 30 pp.

Pamphlet by "Rev." Pastfield, sometime lecturer at naval war college; on technical aspects, armor and gunnery.

343 Patterson, A. Temple. BIOGRAPHY OF ADMIRAL SIR ERNLE CHATFIELD. Projected.

Status unknown, Patterson died in 1983; working on this biography of very important figure in the battle and at the Admiralty.

344 Patterson, A. Temple. JELLICOE: A BIOGRAPHY. London: Macmillan; New York: St. Martins, 1969, 277 pp.

By an academic, University of Southampton; previous biographies by naval officer-friends, Altham [4] and Bacon [12]; chapters 5 and 6 on Jutland, 10 on the Jutland controversy, pp. 99–153, 230–54; later biography by Winton [496]; praised Marder's coverage [297]; stressed Jellicoe's caution; no new information.

345 Patterson, A. Temple, ed. THE JELLICOE PAPERS: SELECTIONS FROM PRIVATE AND OFFICIAL CORRESPONDENCE. 2 vols. London: Navy Records Society, 1966–1968, 840 pp.

Vols. 108 and 111 of Navy Records Society [318] publications; appendix on papers of J.E.T. Harper, pp. 458–90, was an important addition; published here because RUSI decided to release the Harper papers [181] at this time; Jellicoe explained that there was gross neglect from Admiralty intelligence, insufficient information from subordinates at the time of deployment, and he continued to be ill-served except for Goodenough; explained Jutland controversy, which first confronted him when he returned from his Empire Mission: HARPER RECORD [182] withheld; Corbett's NAVAL OPERATIONS [80], which Beatty criticized, thus the Admiralty disclaimer; NAVAL STAFF APPRECIATION [316] from which the ADMIRALTY NARRATIVE [2] was drawn, e.g., Jellicoe concerned about accusations against Evan-Thomas; Jellicoe began second edition of GRAND FLEET [233] with an appendix on Jutland but Cassell did not publish; Bacon's JUTLAND SCANDAL [11] and Churchill's WORLD CRISIS [73], which especially hurt Jellicoe.

346   Patterson, A. Temple. TYRWHITT OF THE HARWICK FORCE: THE LIFE OF ADMIRAL OF THE FLEET SIR REGINALD TYRWHITT. London: Macdonald, 1973, 350 pp.
    Commander of the Harwick Force throughout WWI, cruisers and destroyers operating as defense force in North Sea; Tyrwhitt destroyed his papers; an authentic hero.

347   Pattison, Michael. "Scientists, Inventors and the Military in Britain, 1915–1919: The Munitions Inventions Department." SOCIAL STUDIES OF SCIENCE, 13 (November 1983): 521-68.
    Part of Ministry of Munitions; anti-aircraft research, among other things; little coordination between scientists and military.

348   Pears, Randolph. BRITISH BATTLESHIPS, 1892–1957: THE GREAT DAYS OF THE FLEETS. London: Putnams, 1957, 1979, 214 pp.
    By commander, RN; began with ROYAL SOVEREIGN class of 1890s as first modern battleship, on the DREADNOUGHT, and finally to VANGUARD.

349   Peck, Colin. "Messages Designed for the Enemy: 'Blinker' Hall Fooled the Enemy's Agents on Land and His Ships at Sea." MILITARY HISTORY, 4 (August 1987): 12–17.
    More examples of the work of Room 40.

350   [Pellew, Anthony] "A.P.P." "Something Wrong with Our Bloody Ships." NAVAL REVIEW, 64 (January 1976).
    Article on ship construction problems at Jutland.

351   Persius, Lothar. DER SEEKRIEG. [THE NAVAL WAR]. Charlottenburg: Verlag der Weltbuhne, 1919, 125 pp.
    A German history of the naval war; Skagerrak and a chapter on Scheer and Hipper, pp. 53–64; Persius was critical of German materiel and fleet construction; reply to Persius by a Captain Sheibe, a naval gunnery officer at Skagerrak, in BERLINER TAGEBLETT, 4 December 1918, "How It Happened," in which he denied the claims of Persius: results proved that the German materiel was not inferior.

352   Philbin, Tobias R. ADMIRAL VON HIPPER: THE INCONVENIENT HERO. Amsterdam: Gruner; New York: Humanities, 1982, 231 pp.

Introduction by Keith Bird, who praised the book as an academic biography of a professional leader; note subtitle; Philbin saw Hipper as a nineteenth-century romantic almost too late for his era, thus, the inconvenient hero; Hipper was an outsider, despised by Tirpitz and envied by Scheer; covered five naval battles with much on Jutland; Philbin agreed with Padfield [333, 336, 337] and Preston [362] that British battle cruisers blew up because of unstable cordite and lack of flash protection; disagreed with Marder [297] and agreed with Campbell [61] that German gunnery not so good.

353 Philbin, Tobias R. "Admiral Hipper as Naval Commander." Ph.D. diss., King's College, London, 1975, 396 pp.

On German admiral Franz Ritter von Hipper, 1863–1932, commander of the German battle cruisers and last commander of the High Seas Fleet; Jutland, pp. 244–54, in five phases; Hipper claimed he broke off action because of sun and smoke which at that moment favored the British; he was shifting flagships at the crucial confrontation with the Grand Fleet; Marder [297], Frost [127], Bennett [27, 28], Scheer [410], Raeder [369], Ruge [404], and Doenitz [95] praised Hipper as one of the best tacticians, if not the best, of the naval war; Horn [209] critical of Hipper's role related to the final events and mutiny.

354 Philbin, Tobias R. "IRON DUKE" CLASS BATTLESHIPS, 1911-1943. WARSHIP PROFILE series. Windsor: Profile, 1975.

Pamphlet series; included Jellicoe's flagship at Jutland.

355 Philbin, Tobias R. "KONIG" CLASS BATTLESHIPS, 1914–1919. WARSHIP PROFILE series. Windsor: Profile, 1973.

Number 37 in pamphlet series; on German battleship class.

356 Philpel, Robert H. TO THE HONOR OF THE FLEET. New York: Atheneum, 1979, 459 pp.

A naval novel which began in Washington, D.C. in 1914 and ended at Jutland; involved American naval officers assigned to the British and German fleets prior to the American entry in the war.

357 Pochhamer, Hans. BEFORE JUTLAND: ADMIRAL VON SPEE'S LAST VOYAGE: CORONEL AND THE BATTLE OF THE FALKLANDS. London: Jarrolds, 1931, 255 pp.

Translated by H. J. Stenning; by German first officer of GNEI-
SENAU; one of few survivors of Falklands battle; prisoner of
war; recollections of early phases of WWI.

358   Pollen, Anthony. THE GREAT GUNNERY SCANDAL: THE
MYSTERY OF JUTLAND. London: Collins, 1980, 280 pp.
By son of Arthur H. Pollen to vindicate his father, who was in-
strumental in developing a computer-like central gun fire control
system before WWI, but whose system was rejected by the
Admiralty for one demonstrably inferior—Pollen was later paid
25,000 pounds as a settlement by the Admiralty; Pollen's antagonist was Admiral Sir Frederic Dreyer whose system was adopted;
see Navy Records Society volume on Pollen papers and other
Sumida works [444, 445, 447, 449, 450, 451]; Wilson, Bacon, Dreyer,
and Jellicoe were responsible for rejecting Pollen's "clock" system,
as he called it; some claimed the outcome of Jutland would have
been different if the Pollen system had been in place, thus, the
"mystery" of Jutland.

359   Pollen, Arthur H. THE BRITISH NAVY IN BATTLE. London: Chatto & Windus; New York: Doubleday, 1918, 1919, 368
pp.
Pollen, in addition to his engineering genius, was a journalist,
and this was his history of the war; Jutland, pp. 276–353; Marder
[297] warned to use with extreme caution.

360   Polmar, Norman, et al. AIRCRAFT CARRIERS: A GRAPH-
IC HISTORY OF CARRIER AVIATION AND ITS INFLUENCE
ON WORLD EVENTS. Garden City: Doubleday, 1969, 796 pp.
The definitive history of aircraft carriers; British ships with
reconnaissance aircraft were available at Jutland, but, for various
reasons, were either not used or used and neglected.

361   Poolman, Kenneth. ZEPPELINS AGAINST LONDON. New
York: John Day; London: Evans, 1960, 1961, 334 pp.
Foreword by Sir John Slessor; German zeppelins were available
for reconnaissance at Jutland, but the weather was too bad for
their use.

362   Preston, Antony. BATTLESHIPS OF WORLD WAR I: AN
ILLUSTRATED ENCYCLOPEDIA OF THE BATTLESHIPS OF

ALL NATIONS, 1914–1918. Harrisburg, PA: Stackpole, 1972, 260 pp.

Covered over 300 battleships from 11 nations, 94 from Great Britain; many illustrations; does not supersede Parkes [341].

363 Preston, Antony. CRUISERS: AN ILLUSTRATED HISTORY, 1880–1980. London: Arms & Armour, 1980, 192 pp.

A large contingent of cruisers was at Jutland.

364 Preston, Antony, ed. HISTORY OF THE ROYAL NAVY IN THE TWENTIETH CENTURY. London: Bison; Novato, CA: Presidio, 1987, 224 pp.

Many illustrations, some in color; on Jutland, pp. 32–59.

365 Pridham, Sir Francis. Memoirs. Churchill College Archive Center, Cambridge.

By an admiral, RN; details on the testing of British shells and armor-plating, with results demonstrating inferior quality.

366 Prior, Robin. CHURCHILL'S "WORLD CRISIS" AS HISTORY. Totowa, NJ and London: Croom Helm, 1983, 339 pp.

Ambitious assessment of historical value of Churchill's six-volume history of WWI; concluded: "On balance, Churchill's historical inaccuracies are more than offset by his evident compassion and literary style—but he does seem to have his knife into Admiral Jellicoe!"; chapter 11 on Jutland.

367 PROCEEDINGS OF THE NAVAL INSTITUTE. NIProc. Monthly publication of the U.S. Naval Institute, Annapolis, MD, since 1875.

Timely professional, historical, strategic, and political articles, book reviews, NAVAL REVIEW annual.

368 Pulsipher, Lewis E. "Aircraft and the Royal Navy, 1908–1918." Ph.D. diss., Duke, 1981, 398 pp.

Supervisor was Theodore Ropp; 1909–1911, unsuccessful attempt to develop rigid airship program; need for anti-zeppelin and anti-submarine capability; developments stalled; naval aviators not encouraged by authorities.

369 Raeder, Erich. MEIN LEBEN. 2 vols. Tubingen: Schlichten-mayer, 1956–1957. 1 vol. English ed. MY LIFE. Annapolis, 1960, 448 pp.

Translation by Henry Drexel; by grand admiral, German navy; largely ghost-written by Admiral Erich Forste; on Skagerrak, pp. 64–78, praised accounts of Groos [160] and Frost [127]; jumped into Jellicoe vs. Beatty controversy; Marder [297] praised as good on personalities and on actions in North Sea.

370 Rahn, Werner, ed. DIE DEUTSCHE FLOTTE IM SPAN-NUNGSFELD DER POLITIK, 1848–1985: VORTRAGE UND DIS-KUSSIONEN DER 25. HISTORISCH-TAKTISCHEN TAGUNG DER FLOTTE [THE GERMAN FLEET IN THE REALM OF POL-ICY: LECTURES AND DISCUSSIONS OF THE 25TH HISTOR-ICAL-TACTICAL MEETING OF THE FLEET]. Herford: Mittler, 1985, 236 pp.
Series of essays; study of naval officers of German navy.

371 Ramsay, Sir Bertram H. "Naval War College (Greenwich) Lectures." Jellicoe MSS, British Library.
See Jellicoe MSS [231]; by captain, later admiral, RN, instructor, Senior Officers' War Course, 1927–1929; five lectures presented in 1929; subsequently revised by Godfrey [146]; Marder [297, vol. III, p. 3] quoted from Ramsay: British officers at Jutland "were not educated" to apply the principles of war to tactics. "The whole Navy must bear the responsibility for this."

372 Ranft, Bryan M. "Admiral Sir David Beatty: Commander-in-Chief, Grand Fleet, 1916–1918." Lecture, Society for Nautical Research, 23 November 1989.
By editor of Beatty papers [373] published by NRS.

373 Ranft, Bryan M., ed. THE BEATTY PAPERS: SELECTIONS FROM THE PRIVATE AND OFFICIAL CORRESPONDENCE OF ADMIRAL OF THE FLEET EARL BEATTY. London: Scolar for the Navy Records Society. Vol. I: 1902–1918, 1989, 624 pp.
Vol. 128 of Navy Records Society publications, second volume forthcoming; Jutland, part V, pp. 313–72; some details on Beatty-Jellicoe dispute over disposition of QUEEN ELIZABETH class battleships in Fifth Battle Squadron.

374 Ranft, Bryan M., ed. IRONCLAD TO TRIDENT: 100 YEARS OF DEFENCE COMMENTARY: BRASSEY'S, 1886–1986. Washington and London: Brassey's, 1986, 429 pp.

Centenary volume, 71 articles selected from BRASSEY'S NAVAL ANNUAL.

375   Ranft, Bryan M., ed. TECHNICAL CHANGE AND BRITISH NAVAL POLICY, 1860–1939. London: Hodder & Stoughton; New York: Holmes & Meier, 1977, 178 pp.
Seven scholarly articles by Ranft's research students on interrelationships of technical developments in sea warfare and the evolution of British naval policy, including an article by Ranft, pp. 1–22; noted that RN had no staff and little education and training of naval officers; Alan Cowpe, pp. 23–36, on Whitehead torpedo and RN.

376   Rasor, Eugene L. BRITISH NAVAL HISTORY SINCE 1815: A GUIDE TO THE LITERATURE. MILITARY HISTORY BIBLIOGRAPHIES series, vol. 13. New York: Garland, 1990, 864 pp.
3125 entries of publications since 1960 evaluated and assessed in 500 pages of narrative; on Jutland, pp. 354–56, plus other sections on Marder, Roskill, Kennedy, Anglo-German relations, Fisher era, battleships, battle cruisers, and other warships.

377   Rawson, Geoffrey. EARL BEATTY: ADMIRAL OF THE FLEET. London: Jarrolds, 1930, 256 pp.
Biography of Beatty; conventional approach.

378   Rawson, Geoffrey. JELLICOE. [n.p.], 1933.
Biography of Jellicoe by popular naval historian.

379   Repington, Charles A'Court. THE FIRST WORLD WAR, 1914–1918: PERSONAL EXPERIENCES. 2 vols. London: Constable, 1920, 1201 pp.
A history of the war based on the diaries of this extraordinary figure and prominent journalist-military historian; many references to naval matters; Repington "invented" the term "first world war," meaning the first war to affect all of the world.

380   Reuter, Ludwig von. SCAPA FLOW: THE ACCOUNT OF THE GREATEST SCUTTLING OF ALL TIME. London: Hurst & Blackett, 1940.

By commander of the interned fleet; gave the order to scuttle.

381 Rhodes James, Robert. CHURCHILL: A STUDY IN FAIL-URE, 1900–1939. London: Weidenfeld & Nicolson; New York: World, 1970, 1990, 412 pp.

A study of Churchill's personality during periods of a fluctuating reputation and questionable achievements, including his service the first time as first lord of the Admiralty.

382 Rimell, Raymond. ZEPPELIN!: A BATTLE FOR AIR SU-PREMACY IN WORLD WAR I. London: Conway, 1984, 256 pp.

Foreword by Air Marshal Sir Frederick Sowrey; large picture-book on various British and German forces and the competition between them for control of the air, details on German raids.

383 Rippon, P. M. EVOLUTION OF ENGINEERING IN THE ROYAL NAVY. Vol. I, 1827–1939. Tunbridge Wells: Spellmount, 1988, 304 pp.

By commander, RN; survey of engineering aspects such as propulsion, machinery, ordnance, armor, electrical gear, little on fire control; poorly organized.

384 Robbins, Keith. THE FIRST WORLD WAR. New York: Oxford UP, 1984, 186 pp.

Thematic approach including the land, air, and sea wars; included evaluative bibliography.

385 Roberts, John A. "The Design and Construction of the Battlecruiser TIGER." 2 parts. WARSHIP, 5 and 6 (1978): 2–13 and 88–95.

Details on developments of design and modifications of one of the key battle cruisers; included description of 21 hits and damage experienced at Jutland.

386 Roberts, John A. "INVINCIBLE" CLASS BATTLECRUIS-ERS. WARSHIP MONOGRAPH series. London: Conway, 1972, 50 pp.

Pamphlet series; INVINCIBLE blew up at Jutland.

387 Robertson, Rodrigo Garcia Y. "Failure of the Heavy Gun at Sea, 1898–1922." TECHNOLOGY AND CULTURE, 28 (July 1987): 539–57.

Noted dramatic transformation in warships and projectiles but no change in gunnery; in the RN Fisher and Scott led attempt at gunnery revolution, but Jutland proved the failure.

388 Robinson, Douglas Hill. GIANTS IN THE SKY: A HISTORY OF THE RIGID AIRSHIP. Seattle: U Washington P, 1973, 405 pp.

Basic design by Count Ferdinand von Zeppelin; over 160 rigid airships built; used for reconnaissance; Germans used to bomb Great Britain.

389 Robinson, Douglas Hill. THE ZEPPELIN IN COMBAT: A HISTORY OF THE GERMAN NAVAL AIRSHIP DIVISION, 1912–1918. London: Foulis; Hamden: Shoe String, 1962, 1971, 1980, 433 pp.

Important contribution to aeronautical and naval history; Germans led in development and use for peace and war; chapter 11 on Jutland, pp. 139–70; overall insignificant effect on the war.

390 Roskill, Stephen W. ADMIRAL OF THE FLEET EARL BEATTY: THE LAST NAVAL HERO: AN INTIMATE BIOGRAPHY. London: Collins, 1980, 1981, 430 pp.

By one of greatest British naval historians who gained access to Beatty personal papers after the death of the second Earl; now also seen as one of best accounts of Jutland; Beatty did not publish his memoirs; Chalmers [69] published a discreet biography, others by Chatfield [72], Dreyer [98], and Beatty's nephew [21]; the authoritative and definitive biography of this most charismatic, "Nelson-like" naval leader of WWI; details on love affair with his "Emma," Eugenie Godfrey-Faussett; depicted Beatty as dashing fleet commander, arrogant, snobbish, vain, anti-Semitic, and responsible for the decision on the disposition of the naval air corps, "lost" to the RN for decades; included one of the best analyses of Jutland incorporating recent studies by Pollen [358], Sumida [449, 451], and Campbell [61]; Beatty ill-served by his staff, Roskill concluded that inadequate fire control, not inferior shells, was the British problem at Jutland; reviewed Jutland controversy, "that complicated and somewhat unsavoury fracas," including attempts to "doctor" accounts favorable to one side or the other; notorious Marder-Roskill controversy continued in this biography, Marder pro-Jellicoe, Roskill pro-Beatty; see Rasor [376]; for Roskill, Beatty was more decisive and flexible than Marder depicted him, Roskill emphasized fire control, range-finding, and armor protection problems while Marder stressed cordite problems; Roskill did deplore Beatty's attempts to cover up accounts of Jutland; Jellicoe was appalled that Dewar brothers, inexperienced and unknown, were selected to conduct NAVAL STAFF APPRECIATION [316], which was to be Churchill's primary source [73].

391 Roskill, Stephen W. CHURCHILL AND THE ADMIRALS. London: Collins; New York: Morrow, 1977, 1978, 351 pp.

Little on Jutland, some on the Jutland controversy, much on Churchill at the Admiralty and preparation for WWI, and most on WWII; this was the sensational instance of the notorious Marder-Roskill controversy which included disagreements over Jellicoe and Beatty; catalogue of rejoinders to Marder.

392 Roskill, Stephen W. "The Destruction of Zeppelin L.53." NIProc, 86 (August 1960): 70–78.

Zeppelins conducted reconnaissance in the North Sea and annoyed the British; in 1918, Commodore Sir Reginald Tyrwhitt of the Harwich Force experimented with sea-launching of an aircraft from a towed lighter and after several attempts, it worked and the plane shot down zeppelin L.53.

393 Roskill, Stephen W. "The Dismissal of Admiral Jellicoe." JOURNAL OF CONTEMPORARY HISTORY, 1 (October 1966): 69–93.

Recounted "seismic disturbance" of incident in December 1917 when Sir Eric Geddes dismissed Jellicoe as first sea lord; detailed explanations about the "politics," national and naval, of the decision, Jellicoe's deteriorating health and inability to delegate, and an excellent historiographical survey.

394 Roskill, Stephen W., ed. DOCUMENTS RELATING TO THE NAVAL AIR SERVICE. London: Navy Records Society, 1969, 812 pp.

Vol. 113 of series; volume I, covering 1909–1918; second volume promised but not published; on formative period of Naval Air Service; much conflict with army.

395   Roskill, Stephen W. HANKEY: MAN OF SECRETS. 3 vols. London: Collins, 1970–1974, 1978 pp.
Massive research and knowledge in this "Victorian-type" biography; Hankey was extraordinarily influential in the development of British strategy and security between 1905 and 1942.

396   Roskill, Stephen W. HMS "WARSPITE": THE STORY OF A FAMOUS BATTLESHIP. London: Collins, 1957, 319 pp.
Foreword by Admiral Viscount Cunningham; seventh and last WARSPITE, Cunningham's flagship as Mediterranean commander; commissioned in 1915, to Jutland, pp. 96–153, where there was some damage; Marder [297] saw this as a model ship biography.

397   Roskill, Stephen W. "Truth and Criticism in History—and Jutland." NAVAL REVIEW, 45 (April 1957).
Article on Jutland in professional journal.

398   Rossler, Eberhard. DIE TORPEDOES DER DEUTSCHEN U-BOOTE. [TORPEDOES OF GERMAN SUBMARINES]. Koehlers, 1988, 271 pp.
History of 100 years of the German torpedo.

399   Rossler, Eberhard. THE U-BOAT: THE EVOLUTION AND TECHNICAL HISTORY OF GERMAN SUBMARINES. Annapolis: NIP, 1981, 384 pp.
Detailed reference work; full of technical details on advances, 1900–1974; U-boat operations at Jutland were not successful, p. 66.

400   Roth, Jack J. WORLD WAR I: A TURNING POINT IN HISTORY. New York: Knopf, 1967, 160 pp.
Broadly based history, series of essays.

401   Royal United Service Institution. CATALOGUE OF THE LIBRARY. London: RUSI, 1908.

Holdings, papers, publications of RUSI library; dated.

402 RUSI AND BRASSEY'S DEFENCE YEARBOOK. Various titles. Whitehall, London: RUSI, since 1831.

Old BRASSEY'S NAVAL ANNUAL and other variations; see Ranft [374].

403 RUSI—JOURNAL OF THE ROYAL UNITED SERVICE INSTITUTE FOR DEFENCE STUDIES. Quarterly journal. Whitehall, London, since 1857.

RUSI published this journal, research and reference library, conducted lectures and annual addresses, membership network; prestigious professional organization.

404 Ruge, Friedrich. SCAPA FLOW, 1919: THE END OF THE GERMAN FLEET. London: Allan, 1969, 1973, 175 pp.

Translated by Derek Masters; own personal experiences of service in the High Seas Fleet; disposition of the fleet; Ruge was interned seven months; was later vice admiral in West German navy; a highly influential international naval figure.

405 Ruge, Friedrich. "Scapa Flow." NIProc, 85 (December 1959): 76–85.

Ruge was an ensign on one of the 50 destroyers; details on internment and routine, November 1918–February 1920.

406 Ruge, Friedrich. S.M.S. SEYDLITZ/GROSSER KREUZER, 1913–1919. WARSHIP PROFILE SERIES, # 14. Windsor: Profile, 1972. Pamphlet in series.

407 Ryan, William Michael. LIEUTENANT-COLONEL CHARLES A'COURT REPINGTON: A STUDY IN THE INTERACTION OF PERSONALITY, THE PRESS AND POWER. GARLAND SERIES OF OUTSTANDING DISSERTATIONS. New York: Garland, 1987, 229 pp.

From a Cincinnati dissertation, 1976; Repington was an ambitious army officer whose career was ruined in a scandal and who took up journalism, becoming military correspondent for THE TIMES, 1905–1918; precipitated several sensational political affairs before and during WWI, e.g., the Tweedmouth letter and the shells scandal; Fisher called him "skunk . . . and a damned pimp."

408 Salewski, Michael. TIRPITZ: AUFSTIEG, MACHT, SCHEI-TERN: PERSONLICHKEIT UND GESCHICHTE [TIRPITZ: RISE, POWER, FALL: PERSONALITY AND HISTORY]. Gottingen, Zurich, and Frankfurt: Musterschmidt, 1979, 114 pp.
About the powerful navalist and creator of the High Seas Fleet.

409 Sanderson, Michael, ed. NATIONAL MARITIME MUSEUM CATALOGUE OF THE LIBRARY. 2 vols. London: HMSO, 1968–1970, 977 pp.
By the librarian; research guide at an important library center; divided into parts on biography, navy lists, and other reference aids.

410 Scheer, Reinhard. GERMANY'S HIGH SEA FLEET IN THE WORLD WAR. London: Cassell, 1920, 390 pp.
By admiral, commander of the High Seas Fleet at Jutland; battle of "Skagerrak," pp. 133–73, and aftermath, pp. 174–202; opened with ethnic stereotypes: Anglo-Saxons were grasping for unrestricted primacy, materialistic, and fanatics for power and profit, while Prussians-Germans were idealistic, constantly struggling, pure, and with no desire for expansion; detailed account of Jutland; Hough [216] assessed it as egocentric, idio-syncratic, unreliable, execrably translated, but should be read.

411 Schmalenback, D. Paul. GERMAN BATTLECRUISERS "SCHARNHORST" AND "GNEISENAU." WARSHIP PROFILE series, # 33. Windsor: Profile, 1974, 50 pp.
By German naval captain, pamphlet in series.

412 Schmitt, Bernadotte E. ENGLAND AND GERMANY, 1740–1914. New York: Fertig, 1916, 1967, 524 pp.
By then University of Chicago professor, former president of the American Historical Association; an older but important source for the origins and causes of WWI.

413 Schmitt, Bernadotte E. and Vedeler, Harold C. THE WORLD IN THE CRUCIBLE, 1914–1918. RISE OF MODERN EUROPE series. New York: Harper & Row, 1984, 573 pp.
The World War I volume of an outstanding series which began in 1934, this being the volume of the 21 which covered the shortest

time span; Schmitt died in 1969; Vedeler concentrated on the chapters dealing with the Russian Revolution; inordinate amount of coverage on Jutland, pp. 138–47, "the most intense drama of World War I"; presented phases of the battle, noted Beatty's tactical failures, lack of information by him and others to Jellicoe, Jellicoe able to "cross Scheer's 'T' " twice, and concluding with a series of violent night actions; Hipper was the tactical master, Jellicoe and the decision to deploy and turn away praised by most, including German official history [160]; listed failings of RN but insisted that there was no change in the strategic situation; impressive bibliographical survey including Churchill's critique of Jellicoe [73] and Barnett's assessment of the communiqué and results [17].

414 Schurman, Donald M. THE EDUCATION OF A NAVY: THE DEVELOPMENT OF BRITISH NAVAL STRATEGIC THOUGHT, 1867–1914. Chicago and London: U Chicago P; New York: Krieger, 1965, 1984, 222 pp.
   Study of six naval historian-strategists: J. and P. Colomb, Mahan, Laughton, Richmond, and Corbett; all believed the study of the history of naval warfare would yield valuable lessons; C. Lloyd summarized the book as contributors who changed British naval history from a patriotic antiquarian pastime into a serious academic occupation.

415 Schurman, Donald M. JULIAN S. CORBETT, 1854–1922: HISTORIAN OF BRITISH MARITIME POLICY FROM DRAKE TO JELLICOE. London: Royal Historical Society, 1981, 228 pp.
   The authoritative biography of the civilian historian, strategic analyst, unofficial adviser to Fisher and Jellicoe, and official naval historian of WWI; assisted by Brian Tunstall, son-in-law of Corbett; Schurman called it "a semi-biographical, somewhat episodic, history"; unlike Mahan, Corbett advocated a limited strategy of sea power which stressed maintenance of lines of communication; involved in effort to remove Jellicoe as commander of the Grand Fleet but not part of pro-Beatty cabal; Corbett was originally "in the Fishpond" but broke with Fisher over the naval staff issue; Corbett wrote instructions to Jellicoe on the strategy of minimum risk; began official naval history in 1916 and completed manuscript for vol. III, NAVAL OPERATIONS

[80], which included the Jutland account, just before his death in 1922; at first Churchill temporarily delayed the Dardanelles account, then Beatty delayed vol. III, seemingly permanently; details now available in the A. Temple Patterson biography of Jellicoe [344]; Corbett [80], who began as pro-Beatty and shifted to pro-Jellicoe as more evidence became available, and Marder [297], vindicated the methods and actions of Jellicoe at Jutland; Schurman recounted the story of HARPER RECORD [182] and the Dewars' NAVAL STAFF APPRECIATION [316]; with Corbett's death in 1922, his private publisher insisted upon the integrity of his work, so the Admiralty repudiated it and added a disclaimer, concluding that some findings "are directly in conflict with their [the lords commissioners of the Admiralty] views"; see Admiralty MSS PRO [1] Adm 116/2067 for the packet on Jutland.

416 Scott, John D. VICKERS: A HISTORY. London: Weidenfeld & Nicolson, 1961, 1962, 439 pp.

Vickers founded in 1828 and amalgamated with Armstrong in 1927; produced British arms and armaments before and during WWI.

417 Scott, Sir Percy. FIFTY YEARS IN THE ROYAL NAVY. London: Murray, 1919.

Memoirs of the prominent "Fishpond" gunnery expert and original innovator of director fire control.

418 Searle, Geoffrey R. THE QUEST FOR NATIONAL EFFICIENCY: A STUDY IN BRITISH POLITICS AND BRITISH POLITICAL THOUGHT, 1899–1914. Berkeley and Oxford: California UP, 1971, 286 pp.

Several prominent political and social leaders, e.g., Liberal Imperialists, Lord Haldane, Lord Rosebery, Leo Amery, H. G. Wells, and the Webbs, became obsessed with national efficiency and national security; the movement originated with a series of perceived failures such as the Boer War and increasing isolation of Britain; stimulated efforts to reform the army, navy, government, and empire, and create the CID and a new society.

419 Sheehan, James J. "Germany, 1890–1918: A Survey of Recent Research: Bibliographical Article." CENTRAL EUROPEAN HISTORY, 1 (December 1968): 345–72.

Reviewed recent literature; Fritz Fischer "ignited a scholarly controversy of unparalleled intensity"; themes were expansionist character of Germany's war aims, the leadership transformation from Bismarck to Wilhelm II, the triumph of militarism, and adjustment to total war.

420 Sheehan, James J., ed. IMPERIAL GERMANY. MODERN SCHOLARSHIP IN EUROPEAN HISTORY. New York: New Viewpoints, 1976, 282 pp.
Series of essays by prominent scholars such as J. Rohl, O. Pflanze, H. Rosenberg, and W. Mommsen.

421 Sheehan, James J. "The Primacy of Domestic Politics: Eckart Kehr's Essays on Modern German History: Review Article." CENTRAL EUROPEAN HISTORY, 1 (June 1968): 166–74.
Kehr turned to history to uncover present (1920s) discontents in Germany; his monograph [246] on naval expansion was one of the best on Wilhelmian Germany; Sheehan presented an extensive critique of Kehr and his writing.

422 Sillars, Stuart. ART AND SURVIVAL IN FIRST WORLD WAR BRITAIN. New York: St. Martins; London: Macmillan, 1987, 203 pp.
A study of propaganda, culture, and society; 1916 was seen as "the emotional heartland of the war" as conveyed by writers and artists; Jutland was seen as an example, pp. 24–47; government efforts to manipulate through propaganda, and the army had learned better how to do that than the navy: e.g., the Jutland communique in which the German losses were underestimated and British losses were overestimated, all demonstrating the complete lack of understanding of the public's need for accurate, reliable, and up-to-date information; reviewed sequence of events and releases in detail: the communique, Jellicoe's official report, Churchill's follow-up communique, various published illustrated souvenirs of the battle, Beatty put forward as a great hero and a myth was created, and creation of another myth, the heroic Boy First Class John Cornwell of HMS CHESTER who, though mortally wounded, stayed at his post; Cornwell was reburied in a great ceremony, awarded a Victoria Cross posthumously, and became the object of a hero-cult.

423 Simpson, B. Mitchell. WAR, STRATEGY AND MARITIME POWER. New Brunswick: Rutgers UP, 1977, 366 pp.
Series of essays selected from lectures at the U.S. Naval War College, 1952–1974; several critical of A. T. Mahan and his doctrines; pertinent one: Stephen Ambrose, "Seapower in World Wars I and II," pp. 175–95; examples of Tirpitz's battle fleet built at such costs but contributing little to the war effort, and too much emphasis placed in Germany and Great Britain on DREADNOUGHTS, which were of limited use and reduced options; the major breakthrough of the war was underwater warfare and GUERRE DE COURSE; similar evaluative observations made about WWII.

424 Siney, Marion C. THE ALLIED BLOCKADE OF GERMANY, 1914–1916. Ann Arbor: Michigan UP; Westport: Greenwood, 1957, 1973, 339 pp.
Study of economic warfare carried out by Great Britain and its impact on Germany and on neutrals; Germany retaliated with unrestricted submarine warfare; concentrated on early years, nothing on consequences.

425 Smith, Myron J., Jr. BATTLESHIPS AND BATTLECRUISERS, 1884–1984: A BIBLIOGRAPHY AND CHRONOLOGY. New York: Garland, 1985, 722 pp.
Foreword by Malcolm Muir; 5500 citations, ship/battle index, and chronology; information on sources and archives.

426 Smith, Myron J., Jr. WORLD WAR I IN THE AIR: A BIBLIOGRAPHY AND CHRONOLOGY. Metuchen, NJ: Scarecrow, 1977, 290 pp.
Foreword by Stephen W. Thompson; 2035 entries, chronology, and index.

427 Smith, Peter Charles. HARD LYING: THE BIRTH OF THE DESTROYER, 1893–1913. Annapolis: NIP, 1979, 176 pp.
Fisher coined term "torpedo boat destroyer"; good account on origins and developments; see also March [293], Manning [292], and Kemp [248].

428 Smith, Peter Charles. HIT FIRST, HIT HARD: HMS "RENOWN," 1916–1948. London: Kimber, 1979, 335 pp.

Foreword by Vice-Admiral B.C.B. Brooks; dedicated to Arthur Marder; RENOWN was last of battle cruisers; slipshod effort, superficial, no bibliography; emphasis on operations in WWII.

429 Smith, Thomas F.A. "German Accounts of the Principal Naval Actions, 1914–1916." JRUSI, 75 (1916): 909–20.
Early actions in WWI.

430 The Society for Nautical Research. London. Founded 1910.
Publishes MARINER'S MIRROR [299]; interested in seafaring and shipbuilding in all ages in all countries.

431 Sontag, Raymond J. GERMANY AND ENGLAND: BACKGROUND OF CONFLICT, 1848–1894. New York: Appleton-Century; Norton, 1938, 1969, 362 pp.
Demonstrated that Anglo-German competition and conflict existed before Wilhelm II and the more notable period of rivalry; not natural allies, mutual suspicions, and feelings of increasing hostility.

432 Stanford, Peter M. "The Work of Sir Julian Corbett in the DREADNOUGHT Era." NIProc, 77 (January 1951): 61–71.
On the most brilliant naval writer and strategist.

433 Steinberg, Jonathan. "The Copenhagen Complex." JOURNAL OF CONTEMPORARY HISTORY, 1 (July 1966): 23–46.
A past event and a present fear linked; pre-WWI German fear of repeat of British naval attack on Danish fleet without warning in 1807; related to German naval strategy and Tirpitz's famous "risk fleet" theory; actually the panic-situation originated in the 1890s before the German fleet was developed, and, besides, the German interpretation of an attack out of the blue was incorrect; subsided about 1906.

434 Steinberg, Jonathan. "A German Plan for the Invasion of Holland and Belgium, 1897." HISTORICAL JOURNAL, 6 (1963): 107–19.
Supported Fischer thesis [117], a rigid German war plan without political or diplomatic considerations; no hesitation to violate neutrality.

435 Steinberg, Jonathan. "The Kaiser's Navy and German Society." PAST & PRESENT, 28 (July 1964): 102–110.

A different view of the impact of the German navy, other than the international implications; the navy represented middle-class values, the navy was more open to the middle class for careers than was the army; the navy was national and broadly based; some insights: the navy failed, it contributed to disruption of peace, and it reflected middle-class attitudes and ideas.

436 Steinberg, Jonathan. "The NOVELLE of 1908: Necessities and Choices in the Anglo-German Naval Arms Race." TRANSACTIONS OF THE ROYAL HISTORICAL SOCIETY, 5th ser., 21 (1971): 25–43.

An amendment to the basic naval laws adding more capital ships; introduced by Tirpitz for purely technical reasons, but, in fact, there were political and arms race factors; a bold and provocative move; led to British naval panic of 1909; Tirpitz denied acceleration but the British approved eight DREADNOUGHTS for 1909.

437 Steinberg, Jonathan. YESTERDAY'S DETERRENT: TIRPITZ AND THE BIRTH OF THE GERMAN BATTLE FLEET. New York: Macmillan, 1965, 240 pp.

A major scholarly study of the origins and development of the German battle fleet sponsored by Wilhelm II and formulated by Tirpitz; details on Tirpitz's various rationalizations such as "risk fleet theory" and peculiar parliamentary and financial features of the naval laws.

438 Steiner, Zare S. BRITAIN AND THE ORIGINS OF THE FIRST WORLD WAR. MAKING OF THE TWENTIETH CENTURY series. New York: St. Martins; London: Macmillan, 1971, 1977, 180 pp.

An impressive volume in an impressive series incorporating international and domestic factors leading to the war; domestic roots of diplomatic decision-making, "unspoken assumptions," and a brilliant historiographical survey, e.g., analyzing the Fischer [117] and Arno Mayer theses as they might apply to Great Britain; much on Anglo-German naval rivalry, the most emotive issue, German naval laws, rumors of British preventive attacks on

Germany, naval panic, trade rivalry, German suspicions at Anglo-French and later Anglo-Russian naval cooperation, culminating in the July 1914 crisis and British indecisiveness for several days before the cabinet opted for war.

439   Steltzer, Hans Georg. DIE DEUTSCHE FLOTTE: EIN HIS-TORISCHER UBERBLICK VON 1640 BIS 1918. [HISTORY OF THE GERMAN NAVY]. Frankfurt: Societats-Verlag, 1989, 365 pp.
   On Skagerrak, pp. 336–42.

440   Stephen, G. M. BRITISH WARSHIP DESIGN SINCE 1906. London: Allan, 1985, 120 pp.
   136 illustrations; reviewed the "bad" designs such as K-class submarines and armor protection of battle cruisers; interesting but unbalanced account.

441   Stevenson, David. THE FIRST WORLD WAR AND INTER-NATIONAL POLITICS. New York and Oxford: Oxford UP, 1988, 402 pp.
   On the role of civilians in decisions for war or peace, the study of war-aims and peace-aims, and the reasons regional disputes accelerate into global war; none of the war-aims were achieved and the war fundamentally changed the world.

442   Strachan, Hew. "The First World War: Reading List." HIS-TORY TODAY, 32 (March 1982): 60–61.
   Reviewed recent publications on the war; Fritz Fischer [117] initiated revisionism, Steiner [438] and Berghahn [33] applied INNENPOLITIK vs. AUSSENPOLITIK thesis to pre-WWI situations in Great Britain and Germany, respectively, and a series of notable syntheses: Langhorne [262], Kennedy, WAR PLANS [253], and others.

443   Sturtivant, Ray. F.A.A. AT WAR: THE FLEET AIR ARM. London: Allan, 1982, 144 pp.
   Folio size with 233 illustrations, detailed and comprehensive.

444   Sumida, Jon Tetsuro. "British Capital Ship Design and Fire Control in the DREADNOUGHT Era: Sir John Fisher, Arthur Hungerford Pollen, and the Battle Cruiser." JOURNAL OF MOD-ERN HISTORY, 51 (June 1979): 205–30.

An intensively researched analysis of developments at the Admiralty during the first decade of the century, involving design of DREADNOUGHT, and, more importantly in this case, of the battle cruiser, reducing the navy budget, and adopting a fire control system for the long-range big guns of the new capital ships; for Fisher, concerned about reducing the naval budget, long-range tactics and superior speed were decisive while armor was less important; Pollen designed a rangefinder with a computer-like fire control system which was demonstrated to the Admiralty; Bacon opposed all mechanized systems and convinced the Admiralty to adopt the cheaper manual system of Frederic Dreyer; Pollen later collected damages in a settlement of his claims; see Pollen [358].

445 Sumida, Jon Tetsuro. "British Naval Administration and Policy in the Age of Fisher." JOURNAL OF MILITARY HISTORY, 54 (January 1990): 1–26.

Designated "age of Fisher" as 1889–1918, presumably to differentiate from Marder's Fisher era, 1904–1919 [297]; defined administration and policy broadly to include materiel, design, construction, procurement, logistics, personnel, finance, and governance; between 1889 and 1918 there was rapid and sustained expansion of the Royal Navy and Fisher was the preeminent naval administrator, e.g., Fisher in effect formulated naval design and construction for the ships of WWI; decisions were made which affected performance during WWI, e.g., reluctance to incorporate electricity into naval ships and adoption of the Dreyer fire control system instead of the Pollen computer-like system meant poor gunnery performance at Jutland; noted C. Northcote Parkinson's evaluation of bureaucratic expansion and draw-down during and after WWI, e.g., by 1928 there were 30% fewer sailors but 40% more clerks and 78% more Admiralty officials; cited Marder only twice for minor points.

446 Sumida, Jon Tetsuro. "Finance, DREADNOUGHTS, and Social Reform, 1906–1914." Unpublished paper to the Eighth Naval History Symposium, U.S. Naval Academy, September 1987.

Analyzed the financial problems of the Liberal government of 1905–1914; various standards formulated for the number of capital ships needed; naval budget trends were reductions while

still introducing DREADNOUGHT, but in 1909, demand for eight
DREADNOUGHTS plus increased social welfare commitments;
Lloyd George budget of 1909 brought in new sources of revenue;
presented complicated series of figures and concluded that the
Liberal government attained "guns," "butter," and lower taxes
for the middle classes.

447 Sumida, Jon Tetsuro. "Financial Limitation, Technological
Innovation, and British Naval Policy, 1904–1910." Ph.D. diss.,
Chicago, 1982, 306 pp.

Financial crisis around 1904 meant Fisher needed to reduce
naval expenditure and introduce DREADNOUGHTS, including battle cruisers; long-range gunnery and accurate Pollen fire
control system indicated that less armor protection was required
for battle cruisers, but Pollen system rejected and replacement
system, Dreyer, was cheaper, and inferior; meant adverse impact
in subsequent battles, e.g., at Jutland, three battle cruisers lost.

448 No entry.

449 Sumida, Jon Tetsuro. IN DEFENCE OF NAVAL SUPREMA-
CY: FINANCE, TECHNOLOGY, AND BRITISH NAVAL POL-
ICY, 1889–1914. Boston: Unwin Hyman, 1989, 480 pp.

Revisionist monograph by University of Maryland professor
who has intensively researched this pre-WWI period; the themes
were Fisher's efforts to build superior but cheaper capital ships
and the interaction of structural factors such as economics, finance, national security, and technological change, e.g., destruc-
tiveness and range of naval guns, speed of ships, type of propulsion, size of ordnance, the torpedo, Scott's system of "continuous
aim," and Pollen's system of fire control; these factors influenced
performance in battle, e.g., at Jutland during the battle cruiser
phase British scored 6 hits while Germans scored 25 hits during
22 minutes; long, complicated explanation of reasons for this
disparity; defects in British powder and projectiles also were
factors; in the background were descriptions of the serious
schism, Fisher vs. Beresford, in the navy and the deterioration
of Fisher's abilities to run the navy; Dreyer continued to be
supported and promoted; Pollen was convinced his fire control
system was superior and, in 1925, was awarded 25,000 pounds

for plagiarization of the Argo Clock in 1911; in a review Paul Kennedy [250] praised this "extraordinarily impressive piece of detective work" and noted that Sumida put finance and politics into touch with technology and individual idiosyncrasies.

450 Sumida, Jon Tetsuro, ed. PAPERS ON BRITISH NAVAL GUNNERY AND TACTICS, 1899–1925.
Forthcoming as volume in Navy Records Society series.

451 Sumida, Jon Tetsuro, ed. THE POLLEN PAPERS: THE PRIVATELY CIRCULATED WORKS OF ARTHUR HUNGERFORD POLLEN, 1901–1916. London: Allen & Unwin for the Navy Records Society, 1984, 415 pp.
Vol. 124 of Navy Records Society publications; Pollen, 1866–1937, was a businessman who developed a computer-like system for rangefinding and gun fire control for capital ships, but the Admiralty rejected his system; poor performance at Jutland prompted the navy to redesign the Dreyer system incorporating Pollen's techniques; the documents demonstrated that the navy adopted an inferior system, that the fact of private citizen vs. naval bureaucracy was a factor, and that Wilson and Bacon along with Dreyer were the decisive personalities influencing rejection of the Pollen system; see account by son, Anthony Pollen [358], and other studies by Sumida [444, 445, 449].

452 Summerton, N. W. "The Development of British Military Planning for a War against Germany, 1904–1914." Ph.D. diss., King's College, London, 1969.
Focus on era of war staffs and war planning.

453 Sutton, James Edward. "The Imperial German Navy, 1910–1914." Ph.D. diss., Indiana, 1953, 629 pp.
The Anglo-German naval arms race overshadowed all others, the issue was a secondary one in German domestic politics but in Great Britain, where the problem was exaggerated, there was panic and paranoia; the Germans feared an offensive attack which did not happen.

454 Tarrant, V. E. BATTLECRUISER "INVINCIBLE": THE HISTORY OF THE FIRST BATTLECRUISER, 1909–1916. London: Arms & Armour, 1986, 158 pp.

Foreword by Captain C. H. Layman, RN; INVINCIBLE was the first battle cruiser, "Fisher's brainchild," and blew up at Jutland; why?: Jellicoe and Beatty said "indifferent armour protection" and Tarrant agreed, as did Marder, but others, e.g., the director of naval construction, claimed inadequate "flash" provisions; not convincing, ignored recent studies, e.g., Sumida [444, 449] and Campbell [59, 61].

455 Taylor, A.J.P. ENGLISH HISTORY, 1914–1945. OXFORD HISTORY OF ENGLAND, vol. 15. New York and London: Oxford UP, 1965, 1970, 1985, 740 pp.
The standard survey of the period.

456 Taylor, A.J.P. A HISTORY OF THE FIRST WORLD WAR. New York: Berkley Medallion, 1963, 1966, 188 pp.
A good survey by the fascinating and provocative historian.

457 Taylor, A.J.P. "Fritz Fischer and His School." JOURNAL OF MODERN HISTORY, 47 (March 1975): 120–24.
Historiographical survey of this important revisionist school of German history; see Fischer [117].

458 TECHNOLOGY AND CULTURE. THE INTERNATION-AL QUARTERLY OF THE SOCIETY FOR THE HISTORY OF TECHNOLOGY. Detroit: Wayne State UP, since 1959.
Periodical devoted to technological developments.

459 Tennant, Sir William. "Lectures on Jutland." Seven lectures of 1932. Tennant MSS. at NMM.
By commander, later admiral, RN, a revision of Godfrey's lectures [146], delivered at Naval Staff College, 1932; included convenient list of more important signals, British and German.

460 Terry, C. Samford, ed. THE BATTLE OF JUTLAND BANK, MAY 31–JUNE 1, 1916: THE DISPATCHES OF ADMIRAL SIR JOHN JELLICOE AND VICE-ADMIRAL SIR DAVID BEATTY. Oxford: Oxford UP, 1916, 100 pp.
Often called JUTLAND DISPATCHES; early pamphlet with introductory note and official reports of Jellicoe, Beatty, and

the Admiralty; index of ships, persons, and organizations; this was not the type of publication which would appease the public demand for details.

461 Thetford, Owen. BRITISH NAVAL AIRCRAFT SINCE 1912. London: Putnams; New York: Funk & Wagnalls, 1958, 1962, 1968, 1971, 1978, 1991, 479 pp.

400 illustrations, included all aircraft types in alphabetical listing and included technical data; recent sixth edition.

462 Thoumin, Richard. THE FIRST WORLD WAR. New York: Putnams, 1963, 1964, 544 pp.

Edited and translated from the French by Martin Kieffer; a general survey.

463 Till, Geoffrey. AIR POWER AND THE ROYAL NAVY, 1914–1945. London: Jane's, 1979, 224 pp.

Documents of Fleet Air Arm; analysis of influence of aviation on the Royal Navy; RN responsible for a large number of innovations in carrier aviation; narrow view of aviation strictly to supplement battle fleet was held during WWI and interwar period.

464 THE TIMES. Daily newspaper. London.

Obituaries were informative, e.g., Jellicoe, Beatty, Hipper.

465 TLS—TIMES LITERARY SUPPLEMENT. Weekly. London.

Especially helpful with reviews of recent publications.

466 Tirpitz, Alfred von. ERINNERUNGEN. Leipzig, 1919. English version: MY MEMOIRS. 2 vols. London: Hurst & Blackett, 1919, 597 pp.

By admiral, German navy; Tirpitz as important in development of German navy as Fisher was for RN; Jutland in vol. 2, pp. 382–90; description as if the fleets met by accident, the tactical situation was very favorable for the Germans, other vaguely defined events, and the British fleet disappeared by morning.

467 Tirpitz, Alfred von. POLITISCHE DOKUMENTE DER AUFBAU DER DEUTSCHEN WELTMACHT [POLITICAL DOCUMENTS OF THE RISE OF GERMAN WORLD POWER]. 2 vols. Berlin: Cotta, 1925–1926.

Correspondence and papers by the admiral of the German navy on German naval policy, 1905–1918.

468 Trebilcock, R. Clive. "Legends of the British Armaments Industry, 1890–1914: A Revision." JOURNAL OF CONTEMPORARY HISTORY, 5 (October 1970): 3–19.
Accusations then, and especially immediately after the war, that these industries were war-mongerers, corrupt, greedy, and bloated; a literature of vilification arose, but all of it was exaggerated, Trebilcock concluded.

469 Trebilcock, R. Clive. THE VICKERS BROTHERS: ARMAMENTS AND ENTERPRISE, 1854–1914. London: Europa, 1977, 180 pp.
Introduction by Neil McKendrick; detailed research in business records; study of the development of the modern warship and its arms, plus submarines and aircraft; began as flour mill, then steel mill, and then armaments; became foremost arms manufacturer, even beyond Krupp, by 1914; listed late nineteenth-century innovations: torpedoes, submarine, airplanes, airships, and the battle cruiser.

470 Tulenko, Timothy A. "The Life and Career of Admiral Lord Charles Beresford." Ph.D. diss., Duke, 1967.
Biographical study of Fisher's primary antagonist within RN.

471 Tunstall, William C. B., Tunstall, P. M., and Schurman, D. M. CATALOGUE OF THE CORBETT PAPERS. Bedford: Foundry, 1958, 45 pp.
Corbett, 1854–1922; letters and papers while a fellow at Cambridge, lecturer at the Naval War College, and writer of NAVAL OPERATIONS [80], the official naval history of WWI; included press cuttings about Jutland and letters from Fisher, Richmond, the Laughtons, and Jellicoe; the latter mostly concerned Jutland and Corbett's account of it.

472 Turner, John, ed. BRITAIN AND THE FIRST WORLD WAR. Boston: Unwin Hyman, 1988, 165 pp.
Seven essays by experts summarizing the latest scholarship; Bryan Ranft, "The Royal Navy and the War at Sea," pp. 53–69;

for the RN the war was one of paradox and disappointment, the Grand Fleet failed to gain a decisive victory, but Corbett had predicted that naval battles would never win wars, and the navy had ensured that the war was not lost; Jutland involved over 250 ships and there were heavy losses among the 150 British ships, specifically 14 with 6000 dead; quoted Jellicoe to A. J. Balfour: "The whole situation was so difficult to grasp as I had no real idea of what was going on, and we could hardly see anything except flashes of guns, shells falling, ships blowing up, and an occasional glimpse of an enemy vessel"; see elaboration of his problems in THE GRAND FLEET [233]; the most complete treatment was Marder, vol. III [297].

473 TWENTIETH-CENTURY BRITISH HISTORY. 3 issues per year, since 1990. Oxford: Oxford UP.
A new professional journal.

474 Uhlig, Frank. "The DREADNOUGHT Era." NIProc, 82 (December 1956): 1316–27.
A conventional summary.

475 Unsworth, Michael E. MILITARY PERIODICALS: UNITED STATES AND SELECTED INTERNATIONAL JOURNALS AND NEWSPAPERS. Westport: Greenwood, 1990, 446 pp.
Primarily American publications on military and naval subjects.

476 Van der Vat, Dan. GRAND SCUTTLE: THE SINKING OF THE GERMAN FLEET AT SCAPA FLOW IN 1919. London: Hodder & Stoughton; Annapolis: NIP, 1982, 1986, 256 pp.
A "biography" of the High Seas Fleet from the naval law of the late 1890s to the scuttle and salvage operations; 52 of the 74 ships actually sank; misleading title.

477 Venn, Fiona. OIL DIPLOMACY IN THE TWENTIETH-CENTURY. MAKING OF THE TWENTIETH CENTURY series. New York: St. Martins; London: Macmillan, 1986, 240 pp.
Another of the outstanding studies in this series which incorporated the latest methodologies and scholarship; themes of empire, international relations, and oil were linked; for battle

fleets oil propulsion meant a significant strategic advantage; meant governments intervened to search for oil reserves; prior to 1920 the British became increasingly involved in the Middle East, then deferred to the U.S.

478   Wainstein, Leonard. "The DREADNOUGHT Gap." NIProc, 92 (September 1966): 78–91.

There had been no challenge to British sea power after 1805, then, when the Germans began building, the British grossly overestimated the German threat, thus, the naval panic of 1909.

479   Waldeyer-Hartz, Hugo von. ADMIRAL VON HIPPER. London: Rich & Cowan, 1933, 285 pp.

Biography of the great tactician of Jutland; see Philbin [352, 353].

480   Waldeyer-Hartz, Hugo von. Nachlass [Private papers]. Bundesarchiv/Militararchiv.

Hipper's biographer, but no correspondence with Hipper included.

481   Waller, Michael Craig. "The Fifth Battle Squadron at Jutland." JRUSI, 80 (November 1935): 791–99.

By vice-admiral, RN, commanding officer of HMS BARHAM and flag captain to Evan-Thomas at Jutland; "was unfortunately handled with singularly little enterprise" was typical of the criticism against the Fifth Battle Squadron; this was ill-founded and unwarranted; the five battleships were in the assigned formation and location at the beginning of the battle, TIGER failed to repeat a signal to change course, when the signal was finally received the squadron speeded up and opened fire 20 minutes after the battle began; another point was the "turn-in-succession" signal from Beatty which meant that all ships went through the same spot, the signal was obeyed.

482   WARSHIP: A QUARTERLY JOURNAL DEVOTED TO THE DESIGN, DEVELOPMENT, AND SERVICE HISTORY OF THE WORLD'S FIGHTING SHIPS. London: Conway, since 1977; since 1989, an annual.

Editors have included John A. Roberts, Antony Preston, and Andrew Lambert.

483 WARSHIP INTERNATIONAL. Quarterly journal since 1964.
Toledo, OH: International Naval Research Organization.

484 Watton, Ross. THE BATTLESHIP "WARSPITE." ANATOMY OF THE SHIP series. London: Conway; Annapolis: NIP, 1986, 120 pp.
Book in a series; "biography" of battleship in Fifth Battle Squadron at Jutland with detailed schematics and illustrations; severely damaged and went in circles at crucial stage, with 14 killed; in WWII in Mediterranean and at Normandy, decommissioned in 1947.

485 Wegener, Wolfgang. THE NAVAL STRATEGY OF THE WORLD WAR. CLASSICS OF SEA POWER series. Annapolis: NIP, 1929, 1989, 288 pp.
Translation and introduction by Holger Herwig; fundamental survey of German naval strategy celebrated for its "Atlantic vision"; from an appraisal Commander Wegener of the German navy wrote in 1915; critical of Tirpitz's "risk fleet" theory, the obsession for a fleet battle, and admitted, "We never really understood the sea. Not one of us"; Wegener remained in the navy through the 1920s, retiring as an admiral; famous disputes between Wegener and Tirpitz, and Wegener and Raeder later; Wegener died in 1956.

486 Weinroth, Howard. "Left-Wing Opposition to Naval Armaments in Britain before 1914." JOURNAL OF CONTEMPORARY HISTORY, 6 (1971): 93–120.
Covered period from about 1906, naval arms race, threat of invasion, naval panics in Great Britain, and distractions of the Irish question; radical and moderate Liberals opposed naval estimates of 1913; failed to mount successful opposition.

487 Weir, Gary E. "Tirpitz, Technology, and Building U-boats, 1897–1916." INTERNATIONAL HISTORY REVIEW, 6 (May 1984): 174–90.
Related to Tirpitz's appreciation of the potential of the submarine, and that affected other powers; Tirpitz saw submarines as a distraction from his efforts at building a battle fleet; France, U.S.,

and Great Britain more receptive; not until 1913 was a U-boat command created; Germany had 28 submarines in 1914.

488 Weir, Gary E. "Tirpitz and Technology." NAVAL HISTORY, 4 (Winter 1990): 41–44.
Analysis of Tirpitz's understanding of naval matters.

489 Wemyss, Wester. Papers. Microfilm at University of California, Irvine.
By admiral of the fleet, RN, first sea lord at the end of WWI; papers microfilmed by Marder.

490 Williams, Glyn and Ramsden, John. RULING BRITANNIA: A POLITICAL HISTORY OF BRITAIN, 1688–1988. New York and London: Longman, 1990, 547 pp.
An example of the latest treatment of Jutland in a recent textbook; pp. 372, "the Navy failed to win at the battle of Jutland," was the only mention of the battle.

491 Williams, Rhodri H. "Arthur James Balfour, Sir John Fisher and the Politics of Naval Reform, 1904–1910." HISTORICAL RESEARCH, 60 (February 1987): 80–99.
Julian Corbett Prize Essay, 1984; on politics of naval development; Fisher recognized the importance of propaganda and political power and cultivated journalists, e.g., W. T. Stead and J. L. Garvin [see Gollin, 149], and prominent politicians, especially Balfour, prime minister and, then, leader of the opposition; a complicated political situation in the navy, which split over the Fisher revolution, and in the nation; Fisher survived a series of crises until his first retirement in 1910.

492 Williams, Rhodri H. "The Politics of National Defence: Arthur James Balfour and the Navy, 1904–1911." Ph.D. diss., Oxford, 1986.
Dissertation under Sir Michael Howard; Balfour's efforts to influence Liberal naval policies; disunity in Liberal party exploited by Balfour, leader of Unionists; ultimate objective was to remove navy reform from partisan politics.

493 Williamson, Samuel R. THE POLITICS OF GRAND STRATEGY: BRITAIN AND FRANCE PREPARE FOR WAR, 1904–1914. Cambridge: Harvard UP, 1969, 409 pp.

A brilliantly researched monograph on pre-war military and naval planning and the creation of a quasi-alliance between Britain and France; a key feature of the origins and preparation of WWI was the "Entente Cordiale," which was a step toward the make up of the Allied side in WWI; secret arrangements provided that the British would secure the channel and Atlantic coasts of France and the French fleet would concentrate in the Mediterranean, thus, these arrangements influenced the disposition of naval forces of Great Britain.

494 Wilson, Trevor. THE MYRIAD FACES OF WAR: BRITAIN AND THE GREAT WAR, 1914–1918. New York: Basil Blackwell; Cambridge: Polity, 1986, 880 pp.

Important study of British participation and repercussions on society; part VI on Jutland, pp. 283–308; informative on details; noted Jellicoe's caution; only one aircraft aloft, piloted by Rutland; conclusion that Jutland not a great naval engagement but a "non-battle"; nothing changed.

495 Winter, J. M., ed. WAR AND ECONOMIC DEVELOPMENT: ESSAYS IN MEMORY OF DAVID JOSLIN. Cambridge and New York: Cambridge UP, 1975, 305 pp.

The pertinent essay by Roy and Kay MacLeod, "War and Economic Development and the Optical Industry in Britain, 1914–1918," pp. 165–203; Barr and Stroud, a British arms firm, produced optical instruments for the navy, including rangefinders and sights; Germany was the innovator and primary producer of the best instruments, e.g., Carl Zeiss of Jena, and Britain was increasingly dependent on German sources up until WWI; concluded that British failures to maintain advances were due to "failure of entrepreneurial nerve"; see Moss [310].

496 Winton, John. JELLICOE. London: Joseph, 1981, 320 pp.

Winton has dozens of titles, many popular approaches, but this biography was quite scholarly, thoroughly researched, and unusually balanced; 17 untitled chapters and postscript, an obituary for Earl Jellicoe; no table of contents, no footnotes, but extensive bibliography and index; the best and most recent sources were used; Jutland, chapters 11–13 and 17, pp. 175–227, 289–95; Grand Fleet out on 31 May, German submarines waiting in ambush but no attacks, seaplane carrier standing by but overlooked in sortie signal, confusion in Room 40 and incorrect signal that Scheer was in port, and so on for the rest of the battle; surveys the literature: HARPER RECORD [182] and delay; JUTLAND DISPATCHES [460], "a vast mass of undigested facts"; Bellairs [26] (pro-Beatty), Winton assessed as "unreadable and unread"; A. H. Pollen [359], "another unreadable book"; ADMIRALTY NARRATIVE [2] by the Dewars appeared as substitute for NAVAL STAFF APPRECIATION [316] to which Jellicoe objected; Corbett vol. III, NAVAL OPERATIONS [80], more favorable to Jellicoe but unable to publish deciphered German signals, so unable to specify failures at Admiralty and Room 40, Corbett's volume published 1923, but with Admiralty disclaimer; Bacon [11]; Churchill [73], relied too much on NAVAL STAFF APPRECIATION [316], Bacon, et al.; CRITICISM [14]; HARPER RECORD. [182] finally published, "greeted with a great roar of uninterest"; Harper's TRUTH [184], pro-Jellicoe; Lloyd George's WAR MEMOIRS [276], Edward Carson, in newspaper interview, corrected Lloyd George; five-column spread for Jellicoe obituary in THE TIMES, 21 November 1935.

497 Winton, John. THE VICTORIA CROSS AT SEA. London: Joseph, 1978, 256 pp.

Mini-biographies of 124 winners of the Victoria Cross, Britain's most prestigious wartime medal, including Boy Cornwell, 16 years old, at Jutland.

498 Wolfslalt, Wilhelm. DER SEEKRIEG, 1914–1918 [THE WAR AT SEA, 1914–1918]. Leipzig: Hasse & Koehler, 1938, 412 pp.

On preliminaries and battle of Jutland, pp. 180–236.

499 Wolstencroft, Alan. "The Whitehead Story." MM, 59 (August 1973): 345–48.

Robert Whitehead, 1823–1905, invented and developed the torpedo; trained as engineer, to Manchester, Marseilles, Milan, and Fiume, where in 1860, the first design was completed; 1891, set up company in Great Britain, later bought out by Vickers and Armstrong.

500 Woodward, David. THE COLLAPSE OF POWER: MUTINY IN THE HIGH SEAS FLEET. London: Barker, 1973, 240 pp.

By BBC journalist, used German and British sources.

501 Woodward, David. SUNK!: HOW THE GREAT BATTLE-SHIPS WERE LOST. Boston and London: Allen & Unwin, 1982, 168 pp.
130 capital ships from battle of Lissa of 1866 to YAMATO of 1945; included Jutland.

502 Woodward, Ernest Llewellyn. GREAT BRITAIN AND THE GERMAN NAVY. Oxford: Oxford UP, 1935, 532 pp.
Old standard on Anglo-German naval rivalry; emphasis on diplomacy.

503 Woodward, Ernest Llewellyn. GREAT BRITAIN AND THE WAR OF 1914–1918. EUROPE IN THE TWENTIETH CENTURY series. London: Methuen; New York: Barnes & Noble, 1967, 1970, 610 pp.
By distinguished British historian; general account of British contribution only; listed blunders and mistakes.

504 Young, Desmond. RUTLAND OF JUTLAND. London: Cassell, 1963, 200 pp.
British naval aviator, Fred J. Rutland, at Jutland; memoirs, numerous adventures on land, sea, and in the air; pioneer of naval aviation; helped to introduce the aircraft carrier; to America and in 1941 arrested, probably for selling secrets to the Japanese.

505 Young, Filson. WITH THE BATTLE CRUISERS. CLASSICS OF NAVAL LITERATURE series. London and New York: Cassell; Annapolis: NIP, 1921, 1986, 310 pp. Orig.: WITH BEATTY IN THE NORTH SEA.
Introduction by James Goldrick of Royal Australian Navy; "a study of naval life in war"; by journalist who served in LION, Beatty's flagship, 1914–1915.

506 Young, Kenneth. ARTHUR JAMES BALFOUR: THE HAPPY LIFE OF THE POLITICIAN, PRIME MINISTER, STATESMAN, AND PHILOSOPHER, 1848–1930. London: Bell, 1963, 542 pp.
Little on service as first lord; Jutland, pp. 362–64; on communiqué drafted by Balfour: "a completely unvarnished statement of facts," but described by critics as "a catalogue of an appalling

disaster"; Hankey summed up the battle: "From the point of view of grand strategy, Jutland was as sweeping a success as Trafalgar."

ADDENDUM

507   Bond, Brian, ed. THE GREAT WAR AND BRITISH MILITARY HISTORIANS. Oxford: Oxford UP, forthcoming.

A series of essay contributions assessing military history and historians associated with World War I; the essay, "Bunking and Debunking" by Alex Danchev was applicable.

508   Chamberlain, Waldo. "The German Navy Law of 1912." Ph.D. diss., Stanford, 1939.

This point was the last opportunity for an accommodation between Germany and Great Britain in the Anglo-German naval arms or DREADNOUGHT race prior to the outbreak of World War I; no agreement was reached.

509   Cogar, William B. and Sine, Patricia, eds. NAVAL HISTORY: THE SEVENTH SYMPOSIUM OF THE UNITED STATES NAVAL ACADEMY. Wilmington, DE: Scholarly Resources, 1988, 336 pp.

The published proceedings of the Seventh Naval History Symposium held at the U.S. Naval Academy, November 1986; see the essay "Choosing among Technologies in the Anglo-German Naval Arms Competition, 1898–1915" by Charles H. Fairbanks, pp. 128–38; Fairbanks [514] has contributed significantly to the revisionist interpretations concerning the DREADNOUGHT revolution and critique of Marder [294, 297].

510   Deist, Wilhelm. FLOTTENPOLITIK UND FLOTTEN-PROPAGANDA: DAS NACHRICHTENBUREAU DES REICHSMARINEAMTES, 1897–1914. [NAVAL POLITICS AND NAVAL PROPAGANDA: THE INFORMATION AGENCY OF THE GERMAN NAVY, 1897–1915.] Stuttgart: Deutsche, 1976.

A survey of the Tirpitz era and the connections of politics and propaganda; Tirpitz was a consummate propagandist-navalist.

511   Dorling, Taprell. pseud., "Taffrail." ENDLESS STORY: BEING AN ACCOUNT OF THE WORK OF THE DESTROYERS,

FLOTILLA-LEADERS, TORPEDO-BOATS AND PATROL BOATS IN THE GREAT WAR. London: Hodder & Stoughton, 1931. 451 pp.

Detailed narrative on the operations and actions of the fast British naval warships below cruiser size, generally collectively called "destroyers" at this time and including fast patrol boats, torpedo boats, and torpedo boat destroyers; Chapter 10, pp. 149–240, presented the dramatic, fast-paced operations of destroyers at Jutland.

512   Dunningan, James F. "Jutland." Avalon Hill wargame, 1967, for Thomas Shaw and Avalon Hill Co.

An early electronic simulation wargame, this one, of course, based on the battle of Jutland; Avalon Hill Co. produces a wide variety of wargames.

513   English, J. A. "The Trafalgar Syndrome: Jutland and the Indecisiveness of Modern Naval Warfare." NAVAL WAR COLLEGE REVIEW, 32 (May–June 1979): 60–77.

By a major, Canadian armed forces; a superficial synopsis of concepts of command of the sea and how it was to be achieved; cited theorists Mahan [291] and Corbett [80], and used Marder [297], all applicable to the Royal Navy in World War I: did it suffer from a "Trafalgar Syndome," i.e., was it hurt because of attempts at a decisive victory?; concluded Jutland was "final but indecisive," p. 68.

514   Fairbanks, Charles H. "The Origins of the DREAD-NOUGHT Revolution: A Historiographical Essay." INTERNATIONAL HISTORY REVIEW, 13 (May 1991): 246–72.

A significant contribution in revisionism, generally supportive of the work of Sumida [449] and highly critical of the work of Marder [294, 297]; Marder did not comprehend technical details of naval gun fire control, used shoddy research methods, and was a "Whig" historian, i.e., conformed to a thesis of inevitability; Mackay [287] interpreted Fisher and his contributions to the DREADNOUGHT revolution more correctly and Sumida [449] best of all; most importantly, they incorporated economic and financial factors; financial constraints shaped the naval programmes of Great Britain and Germany; Fisher's real objective was the battle cruiser which fulfilled needs for three previous warship classes and would thus save money; Fairbanks concluded that there was no DREADNOUGHT revolution, only an aborted battle cruiser revolution; the battle cruiser proved to be vulnerable at Jutland; the origins of the DREADNOUGHT revolution were complex.

515 Falk, Edwin A. "British Power since Jutland." YALE REVIEW, 28 (June 1939): 694–718.

A timely but superficial analysis; saw Jutland as a turning point; up to the point of Jutland British naval doctrine had been aggressive and Beatty continued the practice in the first phase but Jellicoe demonstrated extreme caution subsequently; that was the beginning of maritime decline; the post-war Admiralty was dominated by Beatty and repudiated the Jellicoe-dominated, overly cautious version of the history of the battle; if British sea power was to be maintained the Nelson Touch, i.e., aggressive and bold actions, must be revived.

516 Fioravanzo, Giuseppe. A HISTORY OF NAVAL TACTICAL THOUGHT. Annapolis: NIP, 1956, 1979, 261 pp.

Translated by A. W. Holst; by an Italian admiral and tactical expert; emphasis on technological developments and their effect on naval tactics, e.g., the screw propeller and naval aviation.

517 Hansen, Hans Jurgen. THE SHIPS OF THE GERMAN FLEETS, 1848–1945. New York: Arco, 1973, 1974, 192 pp.

Covered the entire history of the modern German navy; a survey of its battle fleets.

518 Herwig, Holger H. "The German Reaction to the DREADNOUGHT Revolution." INTERNATIONAL HISTORY REVOLUTION, 13 (May 1991): 273–83.

Continued revisionism in the tradition of Fairbanks [514] and Sumida [449] and against Marder [294, 297] but as applied to the German navy during the Tirpitz era; there were myths: DREADNOUGHT was built to counter the German threat and Germany was limited because of the narrowness of the Kiel Canal; in the former case, the U.S., Japan, and Russia already planned superbattleships, so Fisher was merely keeping abreast; in the second case, the Tirpitz Plan brought Germany to the verge of bankruptcy and still did not achieve naval superiority.

519 Howarth, David Armine. FAMOUS SEA BATTLES. Boston: Little, Brown, 1981, 185 pp.
Companion to FAMOUS LAND BATTLES, a former publication by the author; selected sixteen naval battles, half from the steam era; included Jutland, pp. 112–27; popularized version.

520 Hughes, Wayne P. FLEET TACTICS: THEORY AND PRACTICE. Annapolis: NIP, 1986.
A synopsis and survey of the matter of operations of battle fleets in proximity to each other, presenting the theoretical and the practical bases; the case of Jutland provoked much comment and reaction.

521 Langsford, A. E. HMS "MARATHON": A NOVEL. Novato, CA: Presidio; London: Barrie & Jenkins, 1989, 1990, 240 pp.
The focus was on Malta and the Mediterranean campaign of World War II but there were recollections of previous times, one of which was an incident at Jutland: the armored cruiser WARRIOR was heavily damaged and sank enroute to homebase; there were some survivors; characters were fictional but the episodes were based on actual events.

522 McKee, Alexander. AGAINST THE ODDS: BATTLES AT SEA, 1591–1949. Annapolis: NIP; London: Souvenir, 1991, 288 pp.
Accounts of twenty-six sea battles during modern times; Jutland, the sinking of BISMARCK, and exploits of Italian frogmen were examples.

523 Ollard, Richard Lawrence. FISHER AND CUNNINGHAM: A STUDY OF THE PERSONALITIES OF THE CHURCHILL ERA. London: Constable, 1991, 192 pp.
Yet another study of Fisher; emphasis on the remarkable contrast between Admirals Fisher of the World War I era and A. B. Cunningham of the World War II era, the link being the career of Winston Churchill; many comparisons and contrasts were developed: Fisher, until the end, got along famously with Churchill; Cunningham could barely abide him; Fisher was not the "Nelson" type, Cunningham was; curiously, although Ollard covered intelligence aspects, he omitted to mention Cunningham's

brilliant use of it, especially against the Italians at the battle of Matapan in 1941.

524 Peebles, Hugh B. WARSHIPBUILDING ON THE CLYDE: NAVAL ORDERS AND THE PROSPERITY OF THE CLYDE SHIPBUILDING INDUSTRY. New York: Humanities; Edinburgh: John Donald, 1987, 210 pp.

The Clyde region of Scotland remained the center of British shipbuilding, civilian and naval, for most of this century; many of the capital ships were constructed there.

525 Pollen, Arthur Hungerford. "Jutland: Before and After." NAVAL REVIEW, 18 (November 1930).

Pollen [359] was ubiquitous and extraordinarily versatile [358]; with his journalist's hat he has assessed THE battle.

526 Pollen, Arthur Hungerford. "Who Lost Jutland?" SATUR-DAY REVIEW, 10 (11 June 1927).

Pollen [358, 359] again evaluated THE battle and presented his assessment.

527 Robison, Samuel Shelbourne and Robison, M.L.C. A HIS-TORY OF NAVAL TACTICS FROM 1530 to 1930: THE EVOLU-TION OF TACTICAL NAXIMS. Annapolis: NIP, 1942, 979 pp.

A comprehensive and detailed analysis of dozens of important naval battles, involving English, Dutch, American, and French forces, among others; Jutland, pp. 852–84, was prominently in-cluded.

528 Tarrant, V. E. BATTLESHIP WARSPITE. London: Arms & Armour, 1990, 160 pp.

A veteran of numerous battles and operations, this QUEEN ELIZABETH class battleship was heavily damaged at Jutland and turned several circles at a crucial point: a well-known incident during the battle; was later involved at Narvik, Matapan, Crete, and Normandy; was again heavily damaged at Salerno.

INDEX

Items that appear frequently throughout this book such as Great Britain, Grand Fleet, battle of Jutland, Germany, and High Seas Fleet are not indexed. Part II, the annotated bibliography, is also not indexed.

About the Author

EUGENE L. RASOR is Professor of History at Emory & Henry College. He has written extensively on British naval affairs. Among his publications are *Reform in the Royal Navy, British Naval History Since 1815,* and *The Falklands/Malvinas Campaign* (Greenwood Press, 1991).

www.ingramcontent.com/pod-product-compliance
Lightning Source LLC
Chambersburg PA
CBHW020354100426
42812CB00001B/60